THE TROSSACH GLENS

Advice to Readers

Readers are advised that whilst every effort is taken by the author to ensure the accuracy of this guidebook, changes can occur which may affect the contents. It is advisable to check locally on transport, accommodation, shops etc but even rights-of-way can be altered and, more especially overseas, paths can be eradicated by landslip, forest fires or changes of ownership.

The publisher would welcome notes of any such changes

THE TROSSACH GLENS

A personal survey of the Trossach Glens

for mountainbikers and walkers

by

Peter D. Koch-Osborne

CICERONE PRESS
MILNTHORPE, CUMBRIA

ISBN 1 85284 199 0
Reprinted 2004

British Library Cataloguing-in-Publication Data.
A catalogue record for this book is available from the British Library.

Mountains are the beginning
and the end
of all natural scenery

John Ruskin

Cover pictures:- Glen Ample

Loch Ard Forest

Index

Introduction

Access to the tracks and paths on the following pages can never be regarded as an absolute right by the cyclist or walker All land is privately owned and it is only the good nature of the landowner that allows us to travel unhindered over his land. In law no such term as trespass exists in Scotland, nuisance or damage has to be proven in order to eject persons from the land but in practice sensible conduct is all that is required to maintain free access. Respect the grouse shooting and deer stalking seasons whatever your views on the subject of 'blood sports'. The author has not once met with any animosity in meetings with estate workers. Your good conduct will keep it this way.

Conservation of the wild areas of Scotland is of paramount importance. Much has been written elsewhere but users of this guide must appreciate that the very ground over which you walk or cycle will be damaged if care is not taken. Please don't use a bike on soft peat paths and tread carefully on other than a stony track. Many of the tracks are in themselves an eyesore and any "development" can cause irreparable damage. Make sure, as walkers and cyclists, we encourage the conservation of our wilderness areas without the pressure of our activities causing further damage. In publishing this book a great deal of trust is placed upon you, the reader, to respect the needs of the region. If all you need is exercise - go to a sports centre! but if you appreciate the unique qualities of the wild places they are yours to enjoy..... carefully! Careless conduct not only damages what we seek to enjoy but, equally seriously, gives landowners good reason to restrict access.

The Maps on the following pages give sufficient detail for exploration of the glens but the Ordnance Survey Landranger maps of the region should also be used if the full geographical context of the area is to be fully appreciated. These maps and the knowledge of their proper use are essential if a long tour or cross country route is to be undertaken.

The mountain bike, or ATB - all terrain bike, has in the author's opinion been badly named. It does not belong on the high tops but is ideal in the glens covering at least twice the distance of the average walker, quietly, whilst still allowing a full appreciation of the surroundings and providing further exploration into the wilderness especially on short winter days. The bike must be a well maintained machine complete with a few essential spares as a broken bike miles from anywhere can be serious. Spare gear is best carried in strong panniers on good carriers. Poor quality bikes and accessories simply will not last. Front panniers help distribute weight and prevent "wheelies." Mud-guards are essential. Heavy rucksacks are tiring and put more weight onto one's already battered posterior! The brightly coloured "high profile" image of mountainbiking is unsuited to the remote glens. These wild areas are sacred and need treating as such.

Clothing for the mountainbiker is an important consideration, traditional road cycling gear is un-suitable. High ankle trainers are best for summer, and light weight walking boots for winter cycling. A zipped fleece jacket with waterproof top and overtrousers with spare thin sweatshirts etc should be included for easily adjusting temperature. The wearing of a helmet is a personal choice, it depends how you ride, where you ride and the value you place on your head! In any event a thin balaclava will be required under a helmet in winter or a thick one in place of a helmet. Good waterproof gloves are essential. Fingers and ears get painfully cold on a long descent at −5°C. Protection against exposure should be as for mountain walking. Many of the glens are as high as English hilltops. The road cyclists shorts or longs will keep legs warm in summer only. In winter walkers breeches and overtrousers are more suitable.

<u>Clothing</u> - for the walker has had much written about it elsewhere. Obviously full waterproofs, spare warm clothing, spare food etc. should be included. In winter conditions the longer through routes should never be attempted alone or by the inexperienced.

<u>Mountainbikers and walkers</u> alike should never be without a good map, this book (!), a whistle (and knowledge of its proper use), compass, emergency rations, and in winter a sleeping bag and cooker may be included even if an overnight stop is not planned. Word of your planned route should be left together with your estimated time of arrival. The bothies must be left tidy with firewood for the next visitor. Don't be too proud to remove someone else's litter. Join the Mountain Bothies Association to help support the maintenance of these simple shelters. It should not be necessary to repeat the Country Code and the Mountain Bike Code, the true lover of the wild places needs peace and space - not rules and regulations.

River crossings are a major consideration when planning long or "through" routes virtually anywhere in Scotland. It must be remembered that snowmelt from the high mountains can turn what is a fordable stream in early morning into a raging torrent by mid afternoon. Walkers should hold on to each other, in three's, forming a triangle if possible. Rivers can be easier to cross with a bike, as the bike can be moved, brakes applied, lean't on then the feet can be re-positioned and so on. The procedure is to remove boots and socks, replace boots, make sure you can't drop anything and cross - ouch! Drain boots well, dry your feet and hopefully your still dry socks will help to warm your feet up. Snowmelt is so cold it hurts. Choose a wide shallow point to cross and above all don't take risks.

Ascents on a bike should be tackled steadily in a very low gear and sitting down wherever possible. While front panniers prevent "wheelies" sitting down helps the rear wheel grip. Standing on the pedals causes wheel slip, erosion, and is tiring. Pushing a laden mountainbike is no fun and usually the result of tackling the lower half of a climb standing up, in the wrong gear or too fast.

Descents on a bike can be exhilarating but a fast descent is hard on the bike, the rider, and erodes the track if wheels are locked. It is also ill-mannered towards others who may be just around the next bend.

Last but not least other users of the tracks need treating with respect - it may be the owner! Bad conduct can only lead to restricted access, spoiling it for us all.

The Maps 1

The maps are drawn to depict the most important features to the explorer of the glens. North is always at the top of each map and all maps, apart from the detail sketches, are to the same scale :- 1km or 0·6 miles being shown on each map. An attempt has been made to present the maps in a pictorially interesting way. A brief explanation of the various features is set out below :-

Tracks :- One of the prime objects of this book is to grade the tracks according to "roughness". This information is essential to the mountainbiker and useful to the walker. With due respect to the Ordnance Survey one "other road, drive or track" can take twice as long to cycle along as another yet both may be depicted in the same way. The authors attempt at grading is set out below :-

metalled road, not too many fortunately, public roads are generally included only to locate the start of a route.

good track, hardly rutted, nearly as fast as a road to cycle on but can be boring to walk far on. Most are forest tracks.

the usual rutted "Landrover" track, rough but all easily rideable on a mountainbike, not too tedious to walk on.

rough, very rutted track nearly all rideable, can be very rough even for walking. Either very stony or overgrown or boggy.

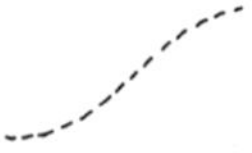

walker's path, usually over 50% is rideable and included especially as a part of a through route. Details given on each map.

The Maps 2

Relief is depicted in two ways. The heavy black lines are now a commonly used method of depicting main mountain summits, ridges and spurs thus:-

Contour lines are also used, at 50m intervals up to about 600m. This adds "shape" to the glens as mapped and gives the reader an idea of how much climbing is involved. Reference to the gradient profiles at the start of each section compares the various routes:-

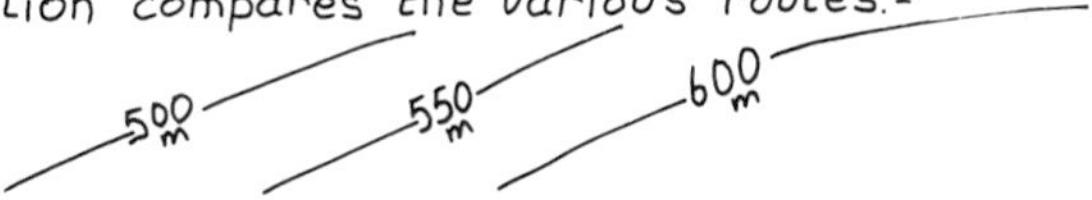

Crags in the high mountains are shown thus:-

....with major areas of scree shown dotted

Rivers generally "uncrossable" are shown as two lines whilst streams, generally "crossable" are shown using a single line. Note:- great care is needed crossing even the larger streams. Falling in can cause embarrassment at best, exposure or drowning at worst. Please don't take risks - besides you'd get this book wet !!

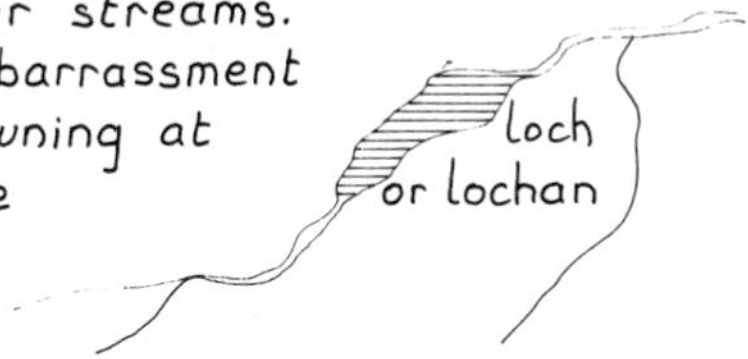

Buildings and significant ruins are shown as a:- ■

Bridges are rather obviously shown thus:-

There are so many trees I wish there were an easier way of drawing them - but there isn't! I'm fed up with drawing trees!!

etc etc .....

Trossach Glens – West

Map of The Trossach Glens showing land over approximately 600m or 2000 feet. A more detailed map of each area precedes each section :– 'Queen Elizabeth Forest Park', 'South Tayside and Lochearnhead', 'Callander to Comrie', and 'Crieff and the Ochil Hills'. Feasible through or 'Link' routes are given in the final section of this book.

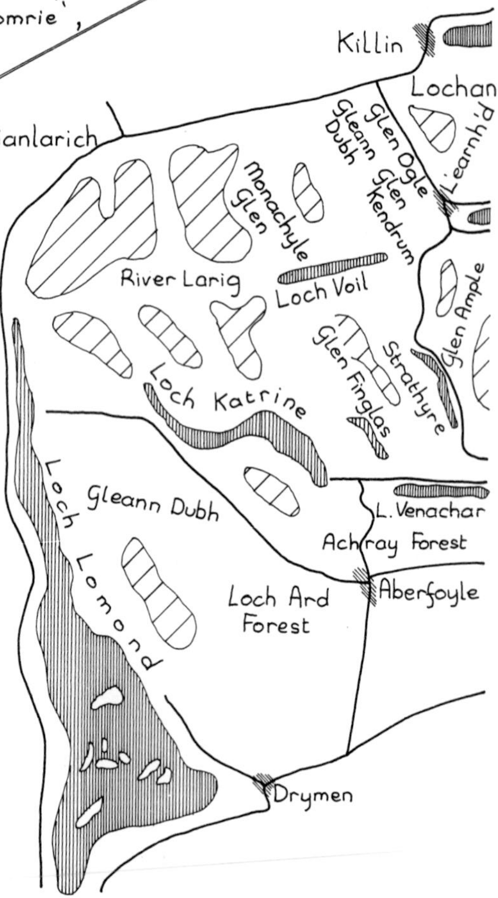

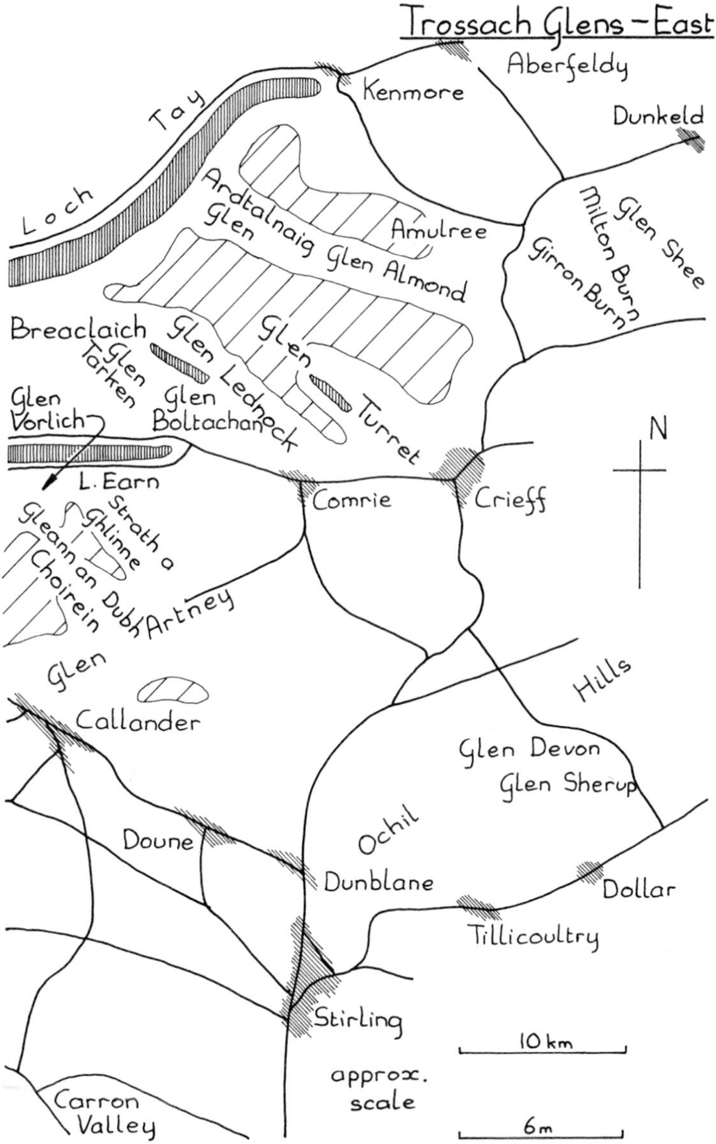
Trossach Glens - East
Aberfeldy
Kenmore
Dunkeld
Loch Tay
Ardtalnaig
Glen
Amulree
Glen Almond
Glen Shee
Milton Burn
Girron Burn
Breaclaich
Glen Tarken
Glen Lednock
Glen Turret
Glen Vorlich
Glen Boltachan
L. Earn
Comrie
Crieff
N
Strath a Ghlinne
Gleann an Dubh Choirein
Glen Artney
Callander
Hills
Glen Devon
Glen Sherup
Ochil
Doune
Dunblane
Dollar
Tillicoultry
Stirling
10 km
approx. scale
6 m
Carron Valley

Queen Elizabeth Forest Park

Queen Elizabeth Forest Park

Access:- The Queen Elizabeth Forest Park comprises several extensive areas of commercial forest to the east of Loch Lomond. Your author has taken the liberty of including other routes in the vicinity under this heading. The Trossachs lie in the heart of this region. Road access centres around the A84 from Stirling via Callander and north to the A85 Crianlarich - Lochearnhead - Crieff road. A few less busy A and B roads radiate from Aberfoyle, which, together with Callander are the main centres. Rail services between Stirling and Crianlarich are now non-existent, the railways of old however have other uses!
Accommodation:- Tourist information centres at Aberfoyle (open April to October) and Callander (open March to December) will provide details of the many hotels, B+B and self-catering establishments. For those of us on a budget there are Youth Hostels at Rowardennan (Loch Lomond) and Loch Ard. Campsites are to be found at Strathyre, Callander and just south of Aberfoyle.
Geographical Features:- The area provides a delightful mixture of high mountains, lochs, forest and turbulent rivers all within a comparatively small area - hence its popularity! The effect of this is some control over where one can and cannot go; here the results are positive with old railways and forest tracks in abundance. This variety and its accessibility can lead to crowds! The Highland Fault, which runs through, and forms, the Menteith Hills south of Loch Venachar is worthy of study. A visit to David Marshall Lodge, the Forestry Commission visitor centre above Aberfoyle should be included in any visit to the area - not just reserved for a wet day.
Mountains:- The most famous - Ben Lomond -

lies to the west presenting its best side towards The Trossachs. West of Strathyre Ben Ledi and Ben Vane provide a fine day out on the hills, whilst Ben Venue, south of Loch Katrine, is probably less populated. The isolated situation of each of these hills makes for an extensive all-round vista from each.

Rivers:- North of the region is drained by the River Earn which steadfastly remains independent until it flows into the Firth of Tay. Virtually all the remainder of the area is drained by the River Forth, which starts out as Duchray Water and Kelty Water east of Ben Lomond, collecting the River Teith (Loch Katrine, Loch Achray and Loch Venachar) just before Stirling. Only a small area of the land east of Loch Lomond drains into it and thence the Clyde.

Forests:- Loch Ard, Achray and Strathyre Forests are the main mountainbiking areas, an activity thankfully encouraged by the Forestry Commission (and the water authorities). These areas are free of restrictions during the shooting seasons from 12th August through to February. Walking can however (beyond the short F.C. waymarked routes) be a bit tedious.

Lochs:- Loch Lomond, despite its famed 'bonnie banks' provides less opportunity to enjoy its shores than elsewhere. Loch Katrine, Loch Voil, Loch Lubnaig, Loch Achray, Loch Venachar and Loch Ard all have character and charm. Glen Finglas Reservoir is a bit bleak whilst Loch Drunkie in autumn (when cars and crowds have gone) is a gem. Cycling the smooth road around Loch Katrine in the sunshine after a week of rough tracks is a pleasure indeed!

Emergency:- With this book and a little common sense it should be almost impossible to become lost in this area. For those new to mountainbiking - or backpacking this area is ideal, even tame. If you prefer lonely, bleak landscapes - go to Rannoch Moor, which would not be what it is without a beautiful area like The Trossachs for comparison.

Queen Elizabeth Forest Park Routes 1

Loch Lomond

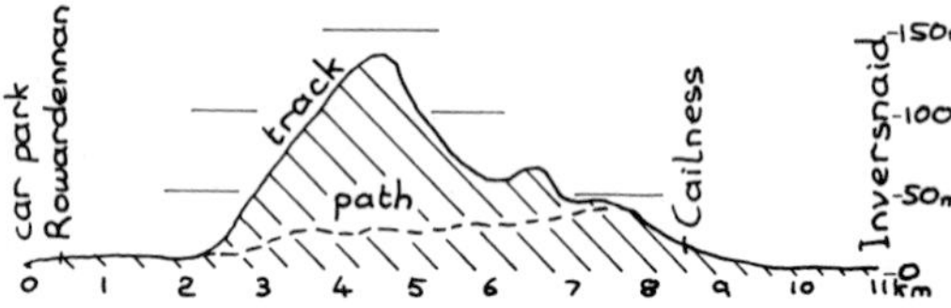

Gleann Dubh

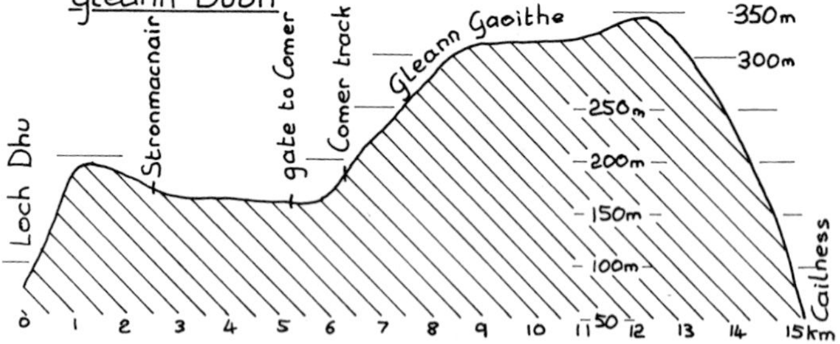

Loch Ard Forest (part of)

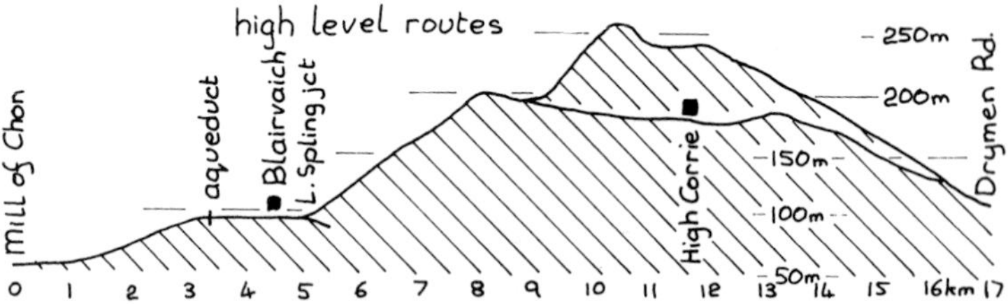

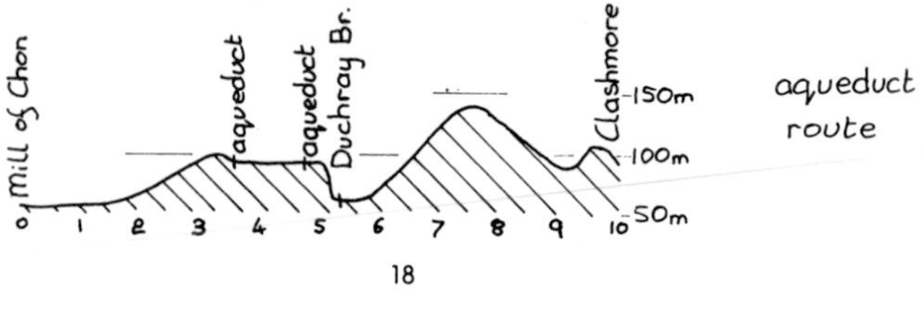

Queen Elizabeth Forest Park Routes 2

Loch Ard Forest (cont'd)

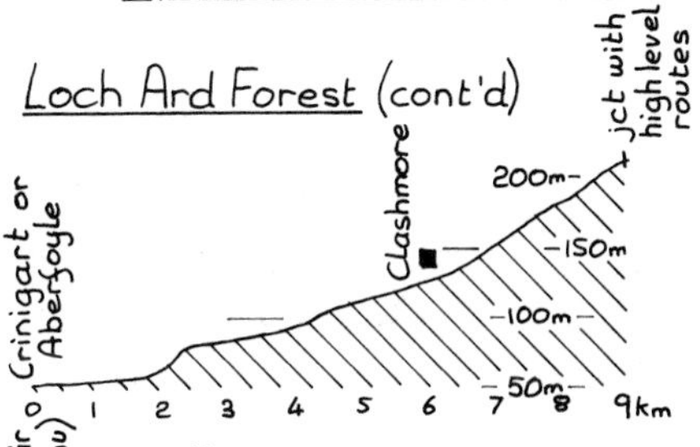

Clashmore tracks (typical profile)

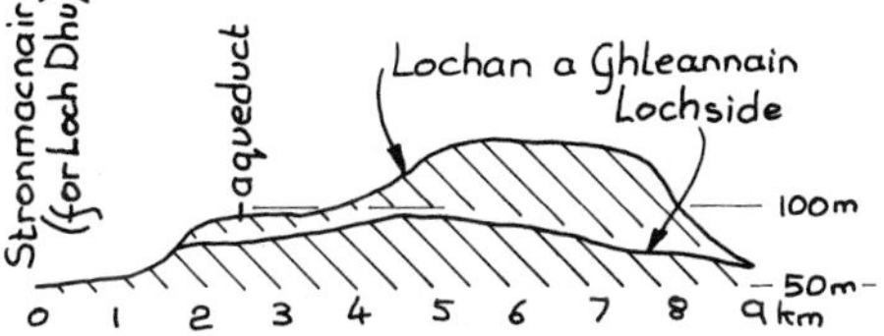

Loch Ard tracks

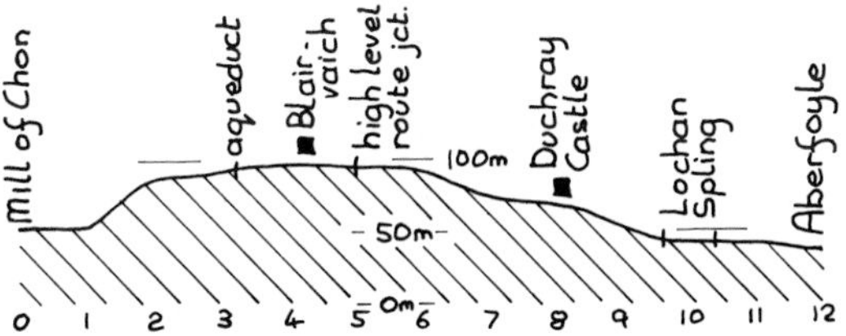

Castle/Lochan Spling

Achray Forest

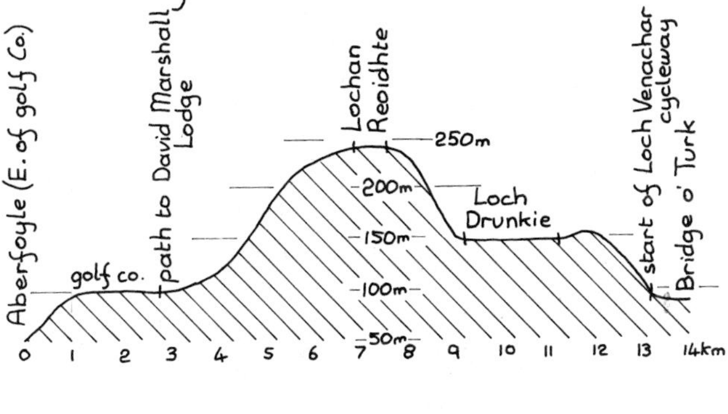

Queen Elizabeth Forest Park Routes 3

Loch Katrine

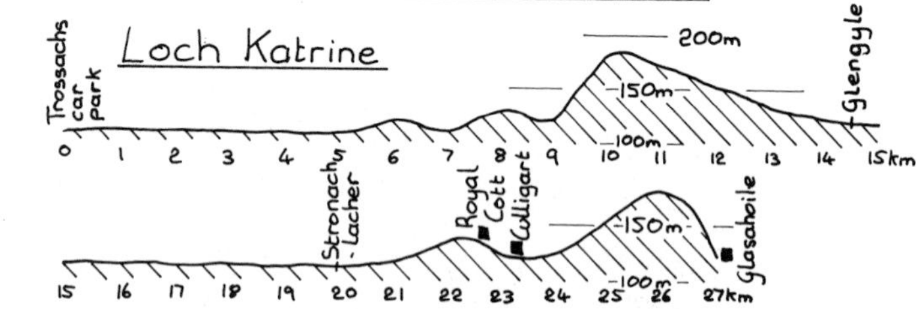

Glen Finglas

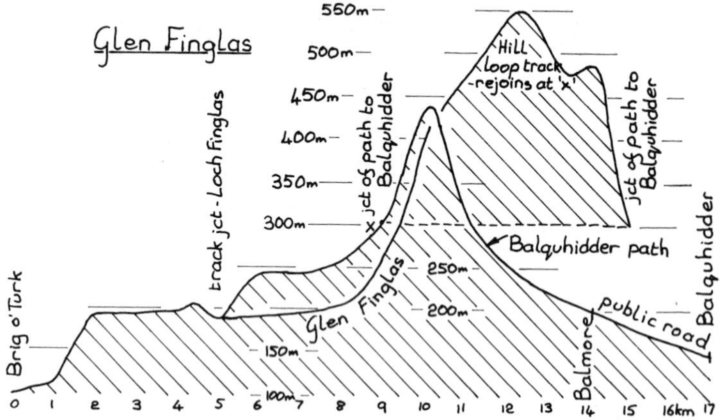

Loch Venachar

-virtually level. Callander to Brig o'Turk is 12km and to Loch Achray, 14km.

Strathyre Forest

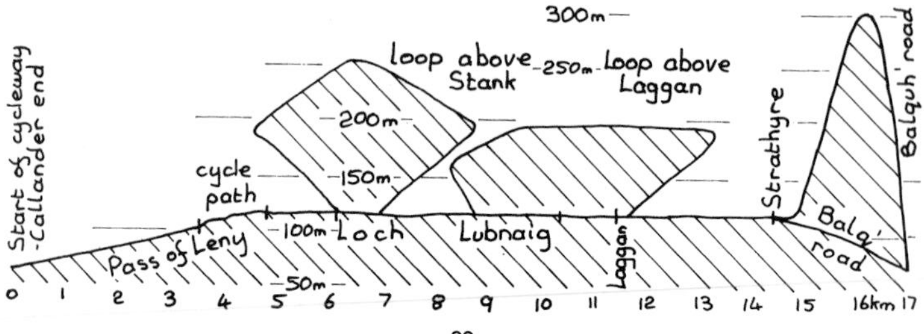

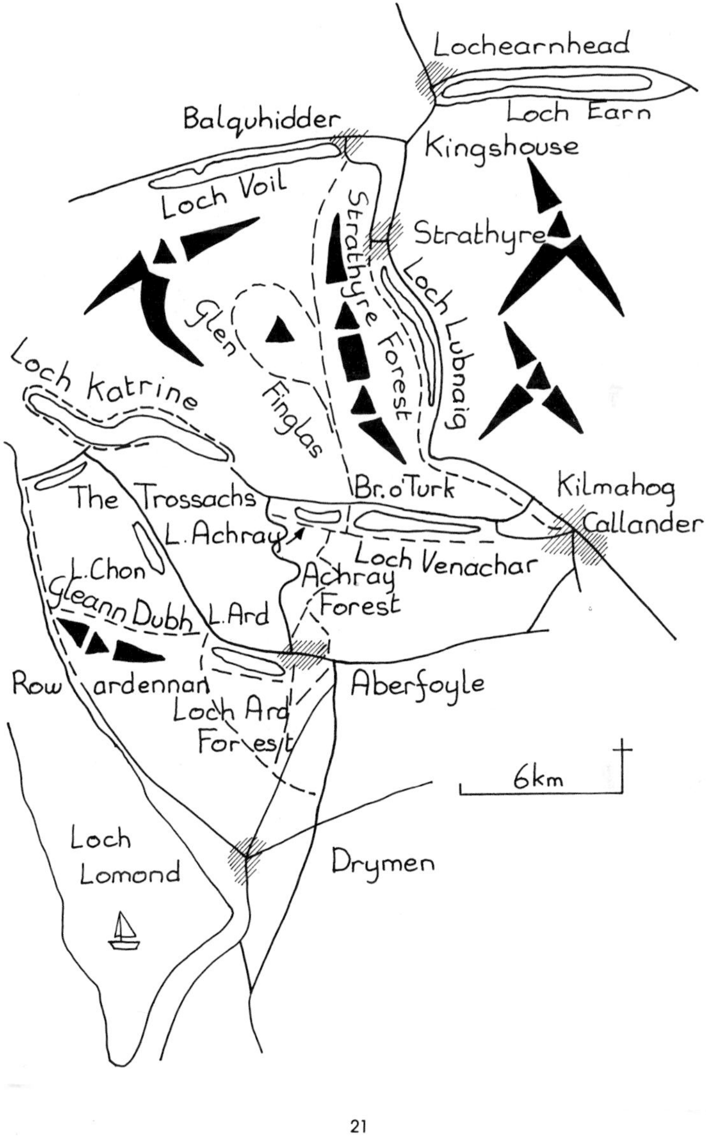
Lochearnhead
Loch Earn
Balquhidder
Kingshouse
Loch Voil
Strathyre
Strathyre Forest
Loch Lubnaig
Glen Finglas
Loch Katrine
Br. o'Turk
Kilmahog
Callander
The Trossachs
L. Achray
Loch Venachar
L. Chon
Achray Forest
Gleann Dubh
L. Ard
Rowardennan
Aberfoyle
Loch Ard Forest
6km
Loch Lomond
Drymen

Loch Lomond 1

↑ Continued Loch Lomond 2 opposite ↑

This section of Loch Lomond has been singled out as it links Rowardennan with both Gleann Dubh (via Gleann Gaoithe) and Glen Arklet. However, both through route possibilities are for walkers only as the track ends before Cailness and the path beyond is too rough for bikes. Also, beyond Comer in Gleann Dubh cycles are banned. (See comments on Gleann Dubh 1). The West Highland Way does of course extend far beyond Inversnaid but this is not another W.H.W. guide! The route depicted makes a fine short excursion. Distance from Rowardennan to Cailness is 9 km (6 m); Cailness to Inversnaid is 3 km (2 m).

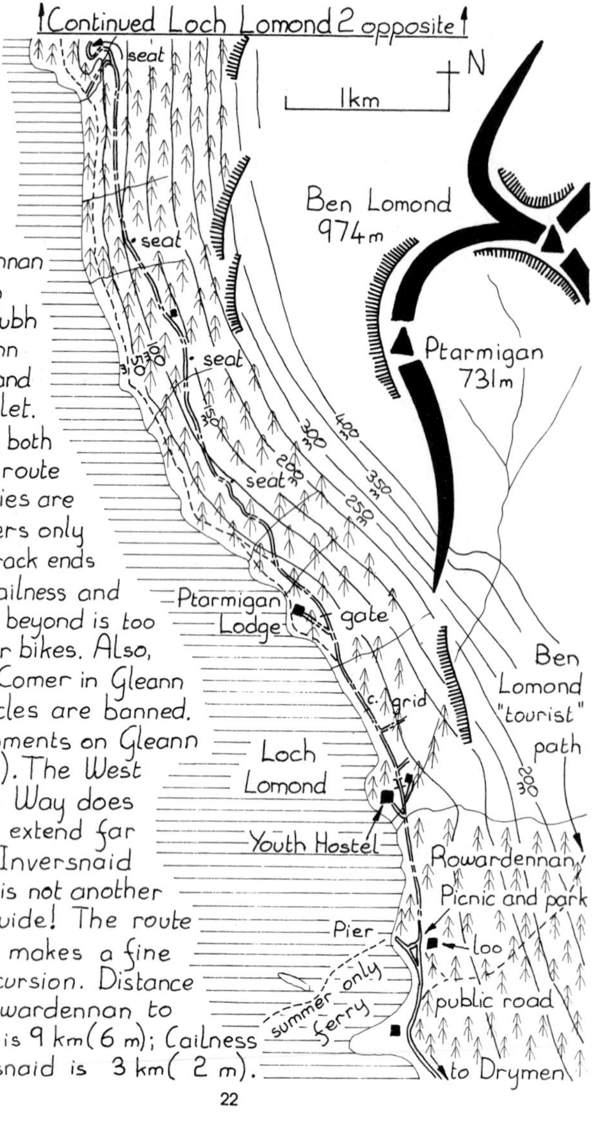

Loch Lomond 2

Here, the procession of weary West Highland Way hikers trudge ever northward (does anyone do it the other way round?) rarely escaping the noise of traffic on the busy A82 road which is within a mile of much of the W.H.W.

There is no proper connection between the W.H.W. path and the Gleann Dubh track at Cailness.

This route has shelter *only* at Rowardennan and Inversnaid.

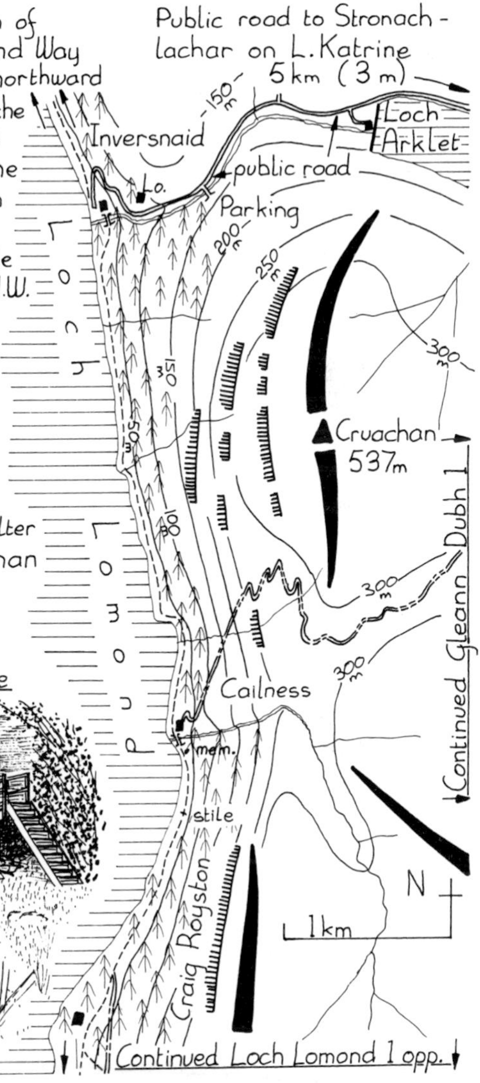

Cailness footbridge

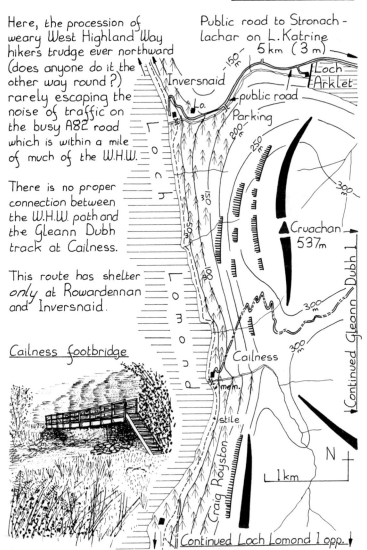

Gleann Dubh 1

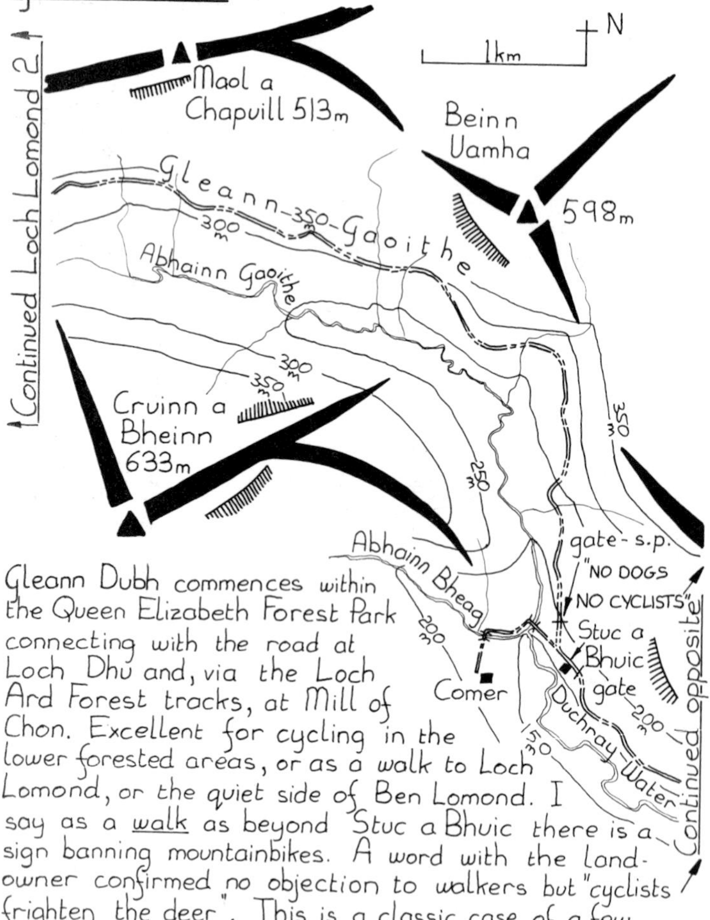

Gleann Dubh commences within the Queen Elizabeth Forest Park connecting with the road at Loch Dhu and, via the Loch Ard Forest tracks, at Mill of Chon. Excellent for cycling in the lower forested areas, or as a walk to Loch Lomond, or the quiet side of Ben Lomond. I say as a walk as beyond Stuc a Bhuic there is a sign banning mountainbikes. A word with the land-owner confirmed no objection to walkers but "cyclists frighten the deer". This is a classic case of a few irresponsible people spoiling some good mountainbiking for the well behaved majority. If mountainbikers were the most pleasant, sensible people on earth free access would continue to be tolerated in most areas. If not, then these are the consequences. Bang goes a "Circuit of Ben Lomond" cycle route. Thanks a lot!!

Gleann Dubh 2

The gate to Comer - Ben Lomond beyond to the Left (S.W.)

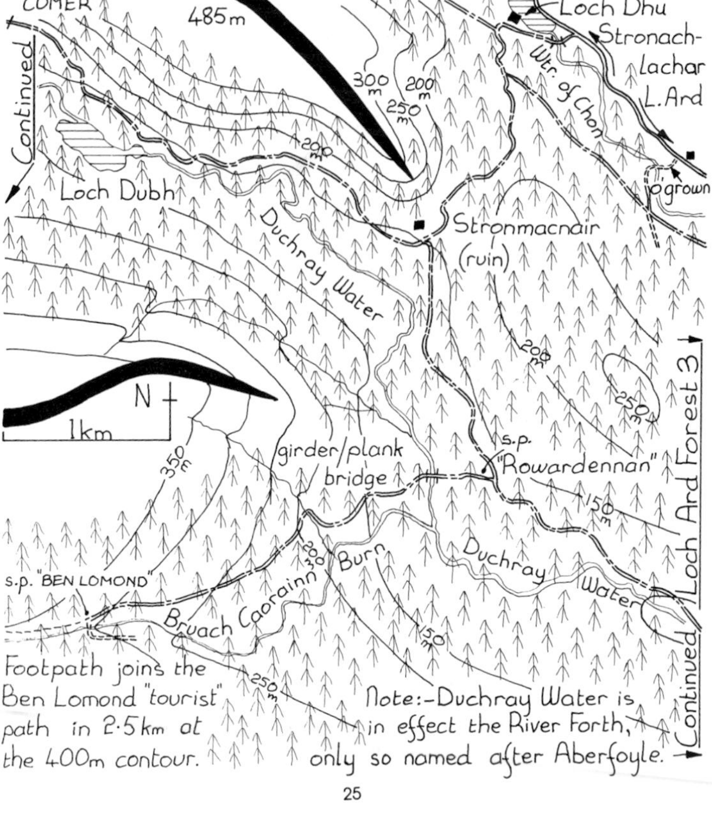

Loch Ard Forest 1

Loch Ard Forest lies to the south west of Aberfoyle and provides, courtesy of the Forestry Commission, an extensive network of tracks covering the southern banks of Duchray Water and the low hills between the northern bank and Loch Ard. Connected with Gleann Dubh, there is road access at Mill of Chon ; Milton ; just west of Aberfoyle ; Crinigart ; Drymen Road, and its link to the A81. At least a couple of days can be devoted to exploring all the tracks by bike - or on foot, but the upper tracks may be of less interest to the walker. Signposted walks are given at Drymen Road, Crinigart and Milton. The purpose of these maps is for more extended exploration. The table below gives a rough idea of the distances involved but the almost infinite variety of available routes makes this very approximate.

	A81 (Hoish)	Drymen Road	Crinigart	Aberfoyle	Milton	Mill of Chon
Mill of Chon	21 (13)	17 (10)	13 (8)	11 (7)	9 (6)	
Milton	22 (13)*	18 (11)*	16 (10)*	15 (9)*		9 (6)
Aberfoyle	15 (9)	11 (7)	5 (3)		15 (9)*	11 (7)
Crinigart	14 (9)	10 (6)		5 (3)	16 (10)*	13 (8)
Drymen Road	4 (2·5)		10 (6)	11 (7)	18 (11)*	17 (10)
A81 (Hoish)		4 (2·5)	14 (9)	15 (9)	22 (13)*	21 (13)

* via Duchray Bridge

distances in km (and miles)

You will be delighted to learn that shelter in Loch Ard Forest is limited to standing in a puddle under an arch of the aqueduct!

Loch Ard Forest 2

The environs of Couligarten and the aqueduct

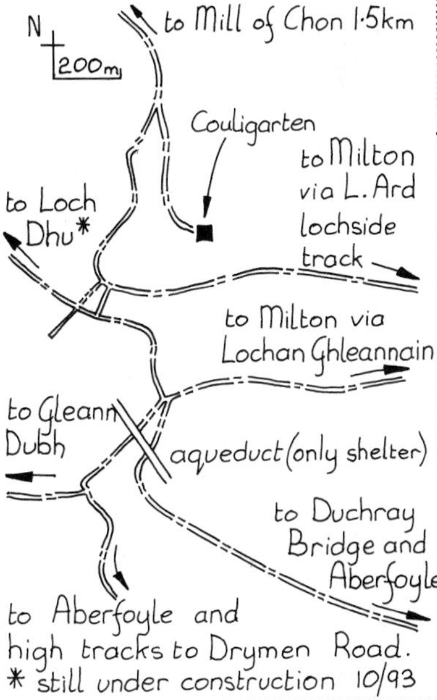

The environs of Clashmore

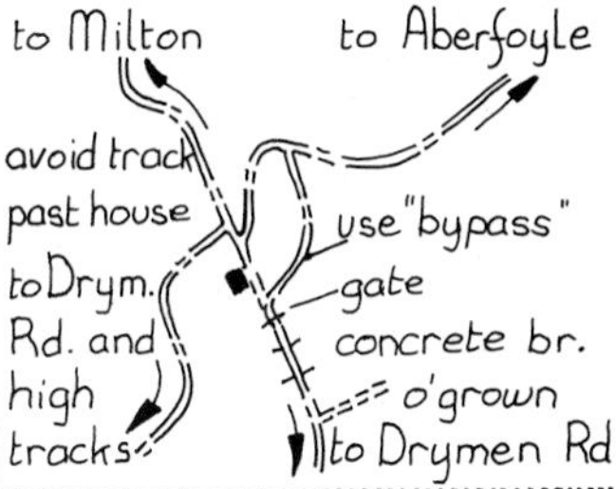

The environs of Milton

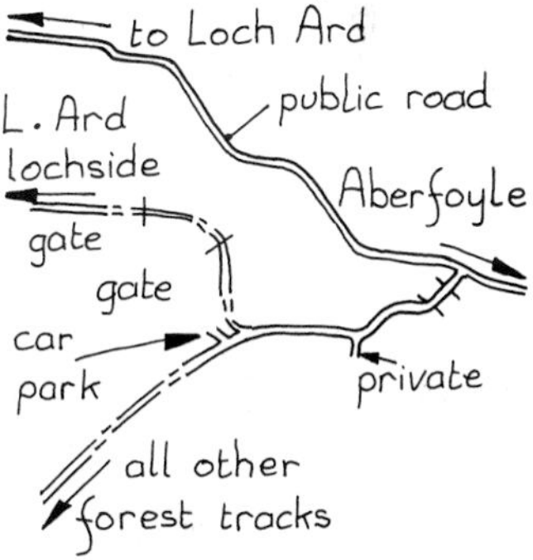

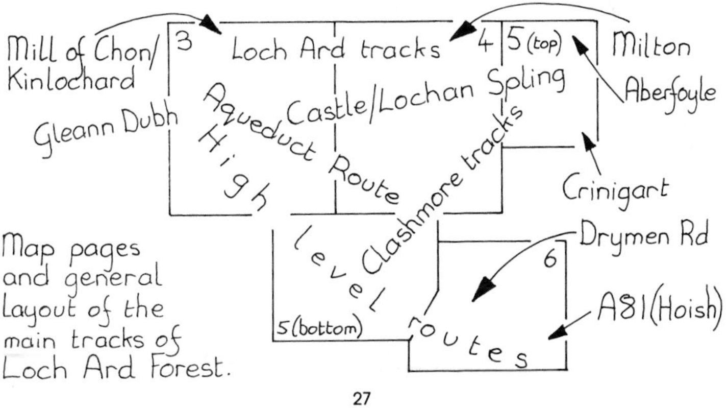

Map pages and general layout of the main tracks of Loch Ard Forest.

Loch Ard Forest 3

Teapot - so named because here tea was brewed to fool the Excise men - they also distilled whisky!

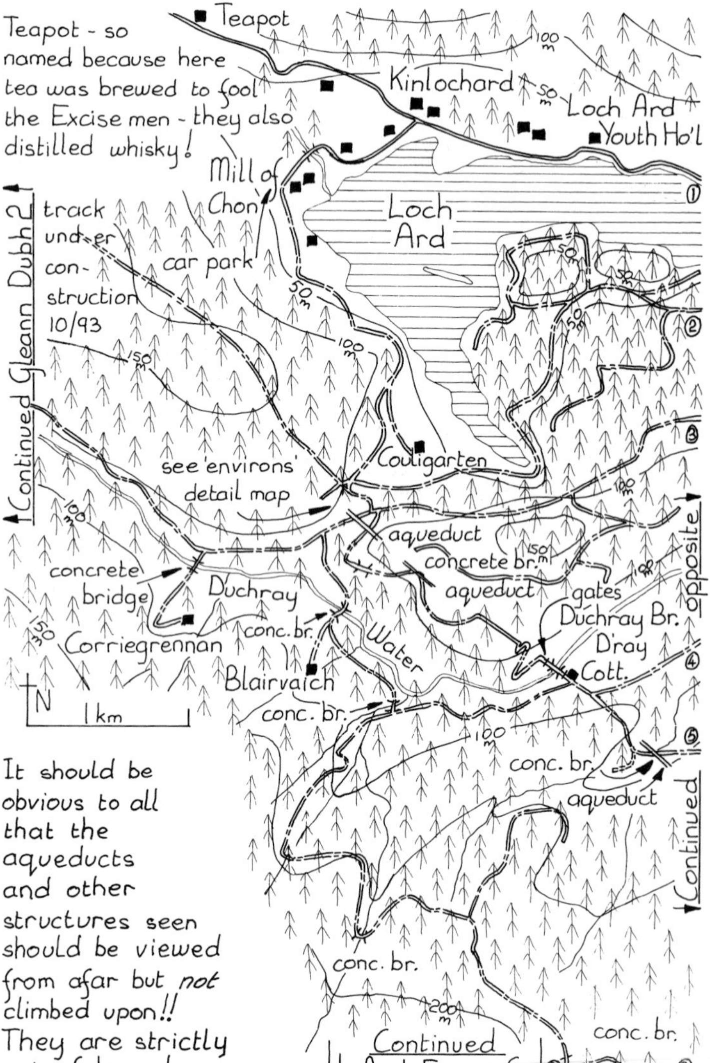

It should be obvious to all that the aqueducts and other structures seen should be viewed from afar but *not* climbed upon!! They are strictly out of bounds.

Loch Ard Forest 4

Loch Ard Forest can either be meticulously explored, noting and identifying each track and landmark or one can safely become gloriously and completely lost, provided of course that some feature is eventually identified in order to find the way out - preferably before dark!

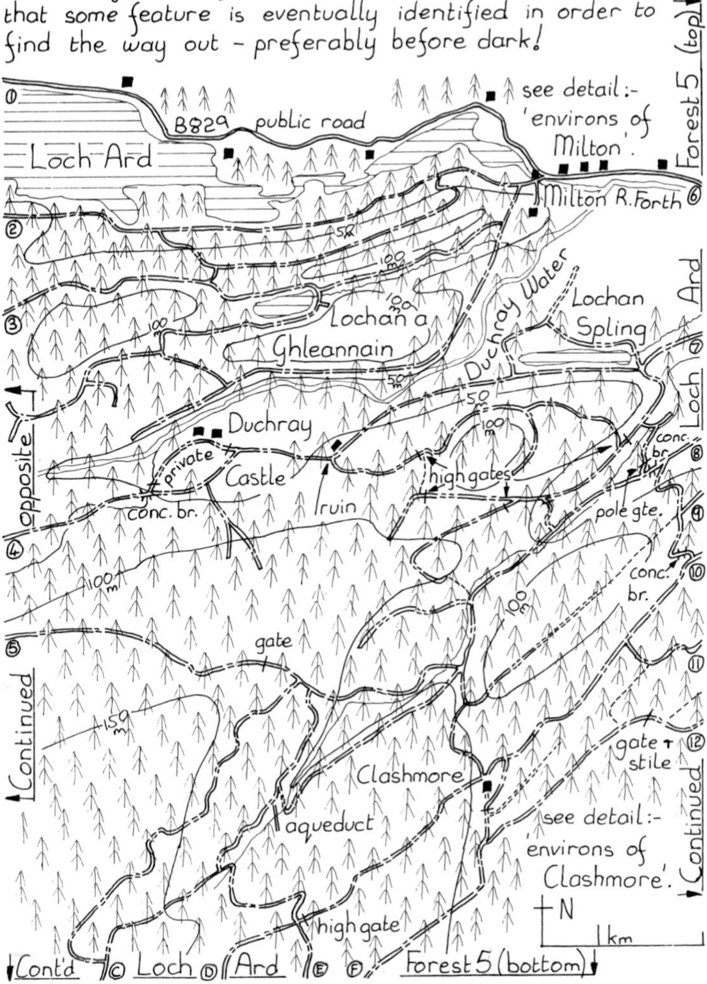

Loch Ard Forest 5

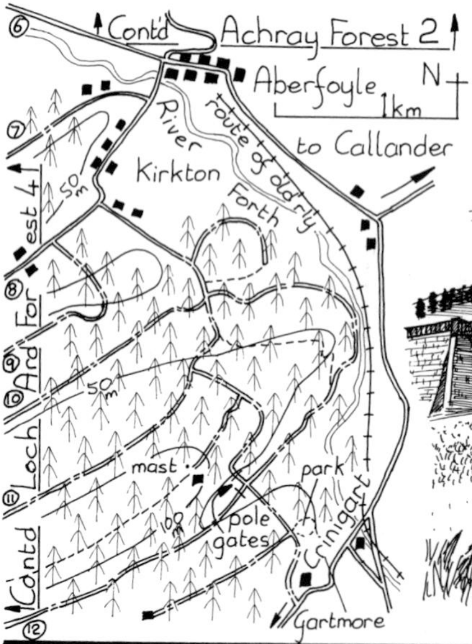

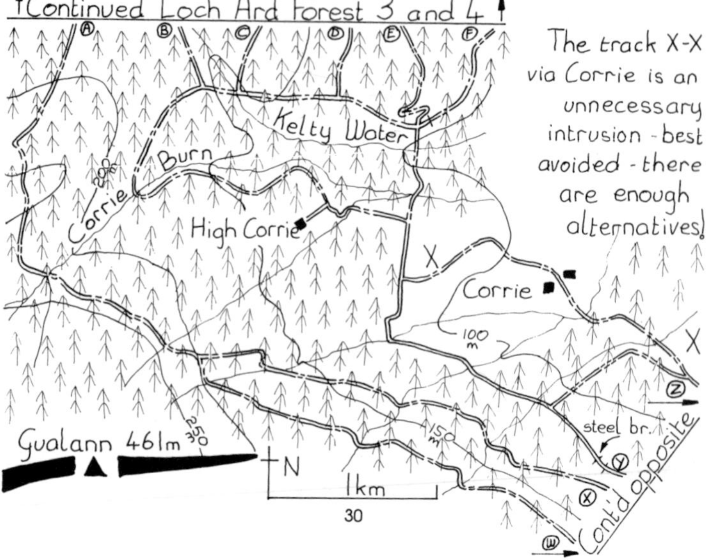

The track X-X via Corrie is an unnecessary intrusion - best avoided - there are enough alternatives!

Loch Ard Forest 6

Ben Lomond stands guard over the tracks of Loch Ard Forest

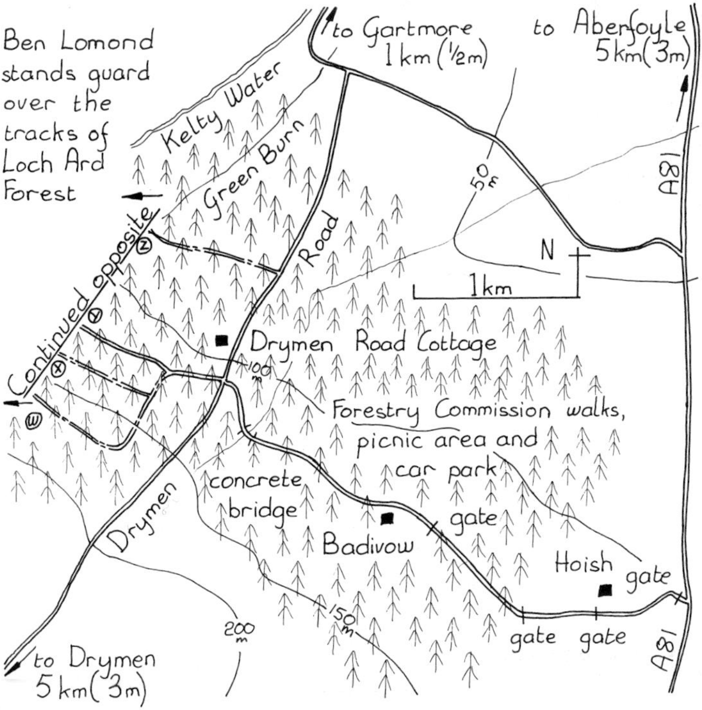

Achray Forest 1

Achray Forest provides the link between Loch Ard Forest and the Loch Venachar cycleway (to Callander), also via Brig o' Turk to Glen Finglas, and (almost) to Loch Katrine. The main tracks, east of Duke's Pass, lie between Aberfoyle and Loch Achray and Loch Venachar, including the picturesque Loch Drunkie. This area is used as the Achray Forest Drive so motor traffic is encountered. Fortunately this provision, for people who just can't leave their cars behind, runs during the summer only. [How one can "experience the forest" from the claustrophobic confines of a motor car is beyond your simple-minded author! Meanwhile the rest of us can experience the noise and pollution only normally available on the roads!] Cars or no cars Loch Drunkie is not to be missed. Surplus energy may be expended on the car-free tracks west of Duke's Pass. There is no shelter (apart from the loo at L. Drunkie) but the David Marshall Lodge visitor centre is worth a visit rain or shine. The Lodge makes a good start/finish point.

Distances :- Aberfoyle to:-

Loch Katrine	16 km	(10 m)
Road by Loch Achray	12 km	(7.5 m)
Loch V. cycleway (start)	11 km	(7 m)
Callander (by Loch D. tracks)	21 km	(13 m)
Callander (by hill path	15 km	(9 m)

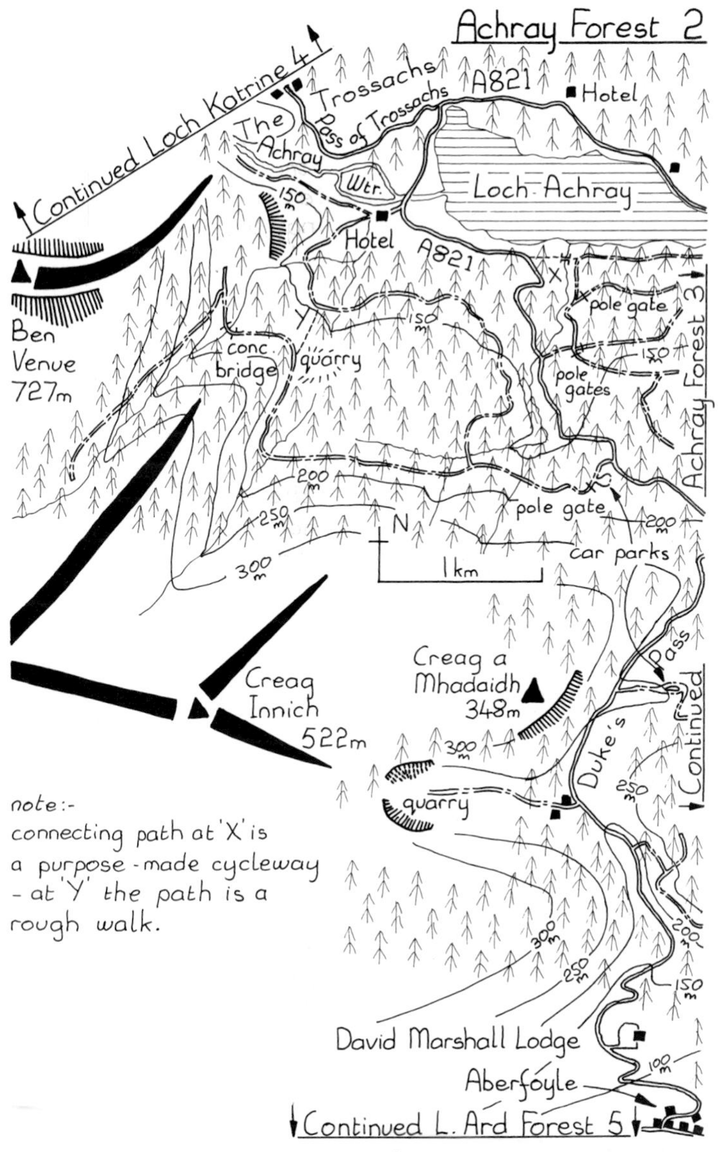
Achray Forest 2
Continued Loch Katrine 4
The Trossachs
Pass of Trossachs
A821
Hotel
Achray
Wtr.
Loch Achray
150 m
Hotel
A821
X
pole gate
Achray Forest 3
Ben Venue 727m
conc. bridge
Y
quarry
150 m
150 m
pole gates
200 m
250 m
N
pole gate
200 m
car parks
300 m
1km
Creag a Mhadaidh 348m
Creag Innich 522m
Duke's Pass
Continued
300 m
quarry
250 m
200
300 m
250 m
150 m
David Marshall Lodge
100 m
Aberfoyle
Continued L. Ard Forest 5
note:-
connecting path at 'X' is a purpose-made cycleway - at 'Y' the path is a rough walk.

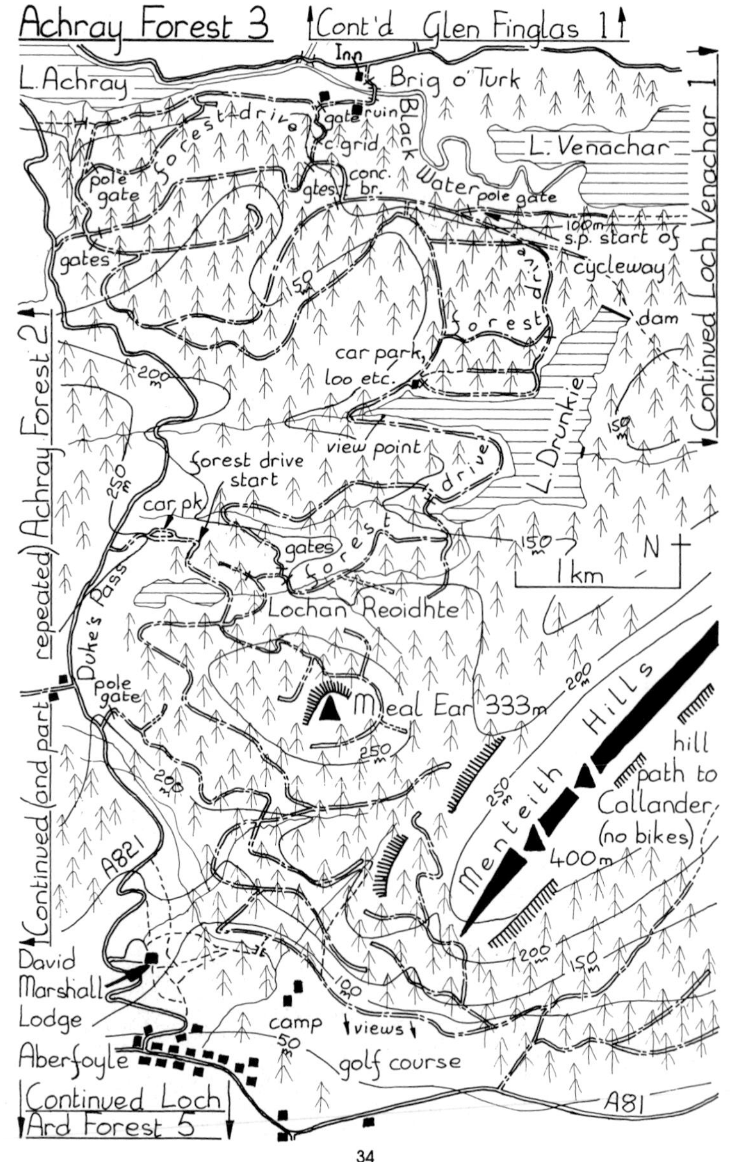
Achray Forest 3
Cont'd Glen Finglas 1
L. Achray
Inn
Brig o' Turk
forest drive
gate
ruin
Black Water
c. grid
conc. br.
gtes
pole gate
L. Venachar
pole gate
100m
s.p. start of cycleway
gates
150m
drive
forest
dam
car park, loo etc.
200m
L. Drunkie
150m
view point
forest drive start
drive
250m
car pk
150m
gates
forest
1km
N
Lochan Reoidhte
Duke's Pass
pole gate
Meal Ear 333m
200m
Menteith Hills
hill path to Callander (no bikes)
250m
200m
250m
400m
A821
200m
150m
David Marshall Lodge
100m
camp
views
50m
Aberfoyle
golf course
A81
Continued Loch Ard Forest 5
Continued (and part repeated) Achray Forest 2
Continued Loch Venachar 1

Loch Katrine 1

The metalled private road along the north shore of Loch Katrine has been designated a cycleway. As a bit of welcome relief from bumpy tracks this route provides a change. An out-and-back run from The Trossachs or Stronachlachar, or an extended ride using the public road past Loch Chon to Loch Ard Forest and Achray Forest makes a round trip for those fit enough. The Loch Katrine road is not entirely free of traffic as limited access to residents etc. is permitted. This series of guide books was nearly brought to an abrupt end when yours truly met the "postie" on a bend - so be alert! A tedious route to walk though many take short walks at The Trossachs end of the loch - indeed these walkers constitute a crowd in summer - care needed with a bike. When the sun shines the scene is one of tranquil beauty, when it doesn't there is no shelter between the pier in the east and Stronachlachar to the west, a distance of 20km (12 miles). The return journey via Loch Chon, Loch Ard Forest and Achray Forest is an additional 40km (25 miles)

Feet up at Loch Katrine

Loch Katrine 2

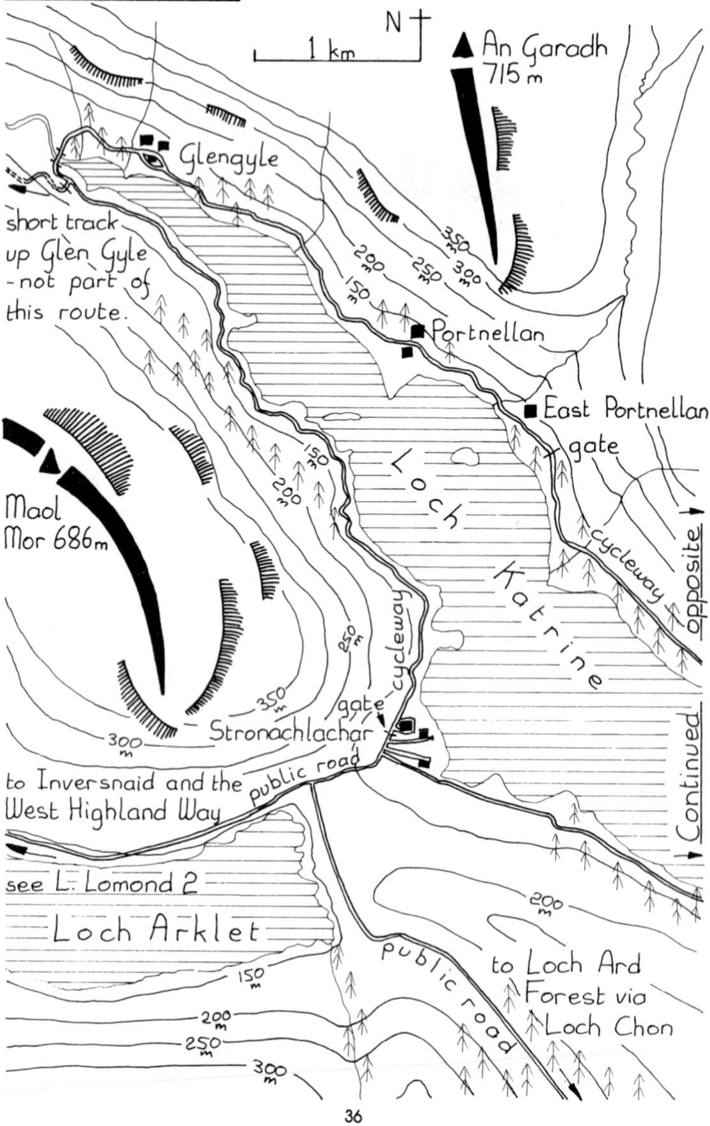

N
1 km
An Garadh 715 m
Glengyle
short track up Glen Gyle - not part of this route.
Portnellan
East Portnellan
gate
Loch Katrine
cycleway
opposite
Maol Mor 686m
350 m
300 m
250 m
200 m
150 m
cycleway
gate
Stronachlachar
public road
to Inversnaid and the West Highland Way
see L. Lomond 2
Loch Arklet
Continued
public road
to Loch Ard Forest via Loch Chon

Loch Katrine 3

The pier building
Stronachlachar

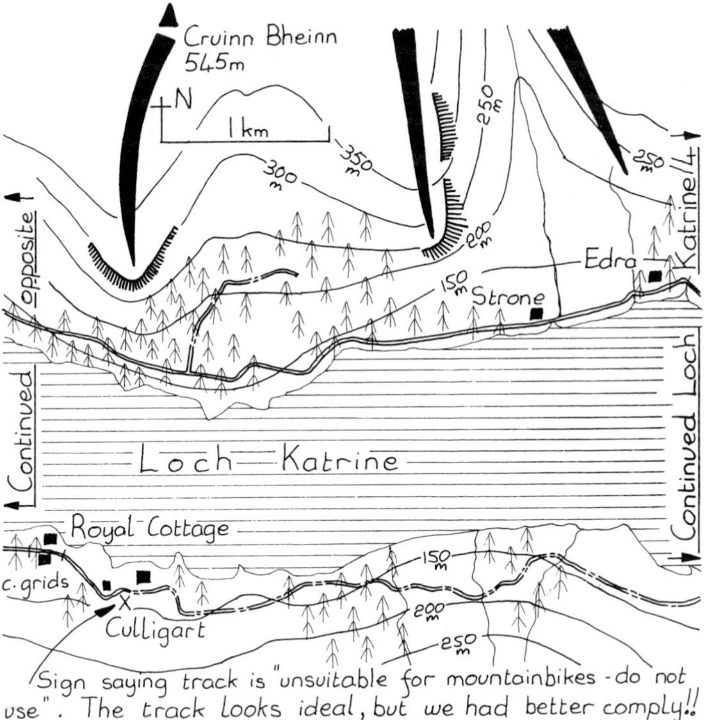

Sign saying track is "unsuitable for mountainbikes - do not use". The track looks ideal, but we had better comply!! A more honest reason for the ban would be appreciated.

Loch Katrine 4

Apologies may be due here (to whom?) for the adoption of The Trossachs in the title of this book as "The Trossachs" is the name given only to the square mile or so at the outlet of Loch Katrine. However, this name has assumed a fame far beyond its geographical importance and is commonly used to describe a far wider area. Your humble author accepts responsibility for perpetuating this inaccuracy!!

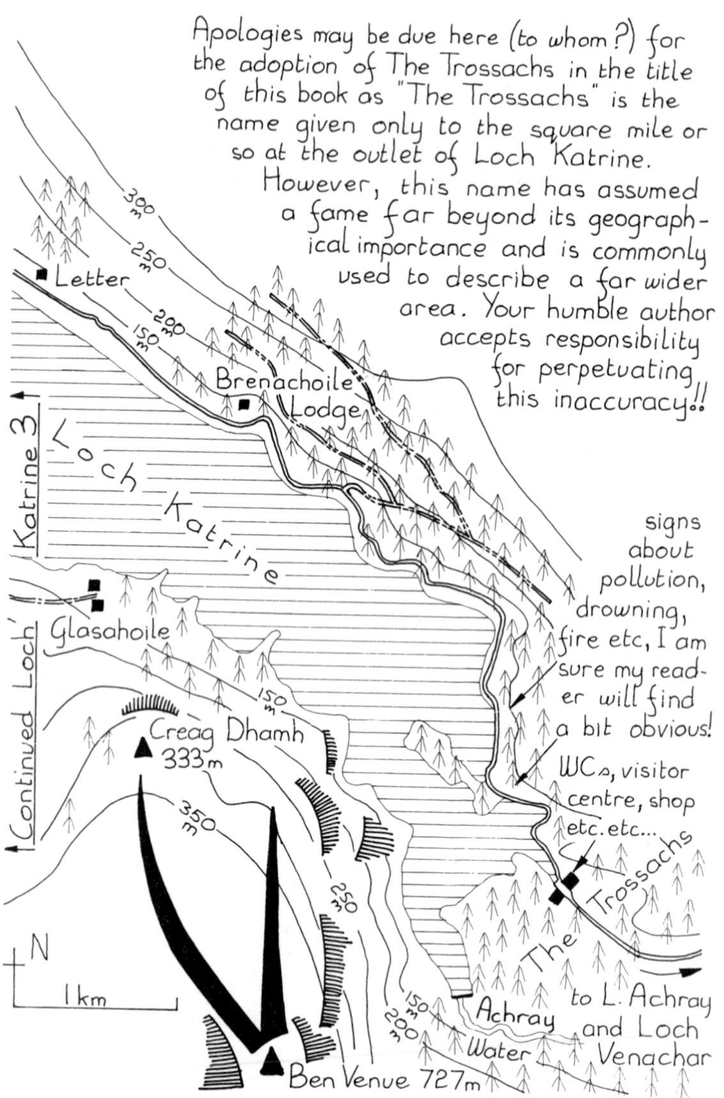

Letter
300 m
250 m
200 m
150 m
Brenachoile Lodge
Continued Loch Katrine 3
Loch Katrine
Glasahoile
150 m
Creag Dhamh 333m
350 m
250 m
150 m
200 m
300
signs about pollution, drowning, fire etc, I am sure my reader will find a bit obvious!
WCs, visitor centre, shop etc. etc...
The Trossachs
to L. Achray and Loch Venachar
Achray Water
Ben Venue 727m
N
1km

Glen Finglas 1

Glen Finglas is an alternative to Strathyre for those en route between The Trossachs or Achray Forest and Balquhidder. A shorter route than Loch Venachar/Strathyre only for those with a serious energy surplus for the climb up to 600m (1950ft) via Glen Finglas, or 420m (1400ft) over the col to Balquhidder. The through route is not a bike ride as part is on an indistinct path. The 'circular' route may be walked or cycled. Once again there is no shelter - not the best route for rough weather.

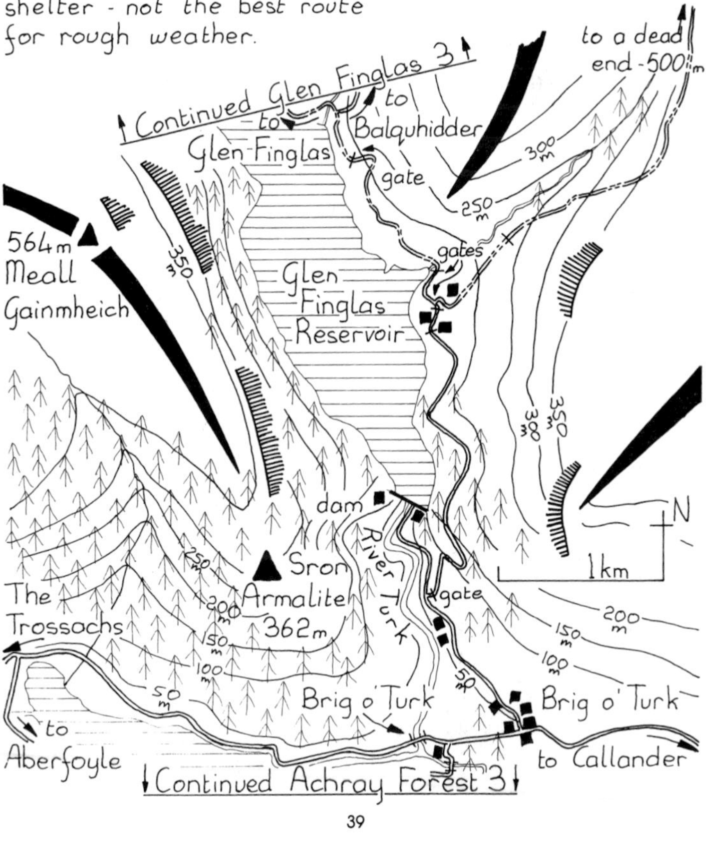

Glen Finglas 2

The climb up the higher reaches of Glen Finglas has been tentatively graded as:- ═══-═══-═══. However, when surveyed this track had been improved and the surface was an unconsolidated and glutinous:- ==========. I hope by the time these words are published that the surface has consolidated with use and the weather. If not, you have been warned and your bike will have to be pushed up the entire climb as mine was!

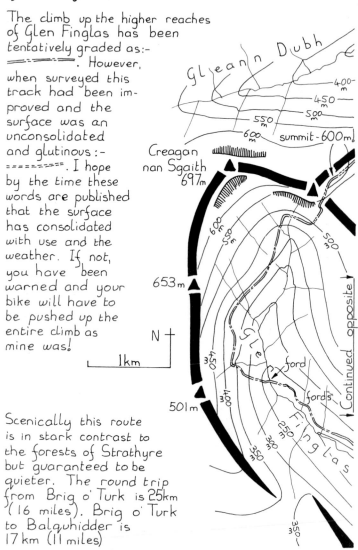

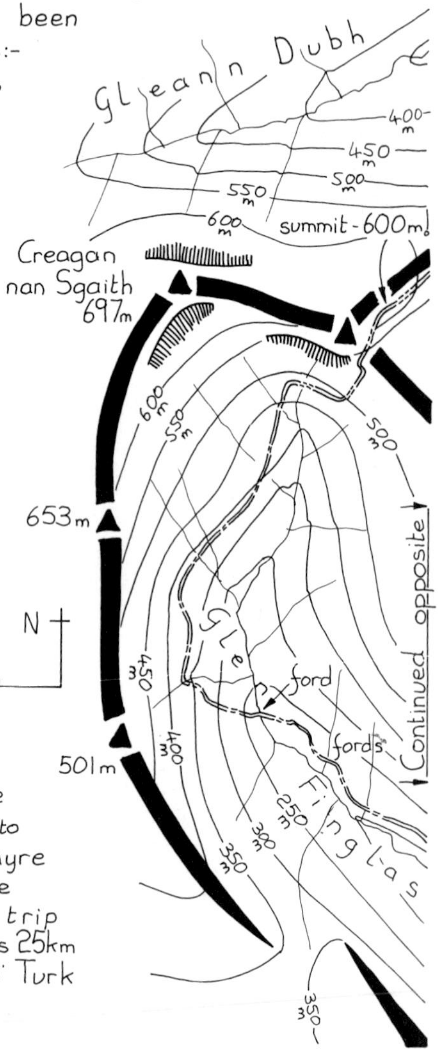

Scenically this route is in stark contrast to the forests of Strathyre but guaranteed to be quieter. The round trip from Brig o' Turk is 25km (16 miles). Brig o' Turk to Balquhidder is 17 km (11 miles)

Glen Finglas 3

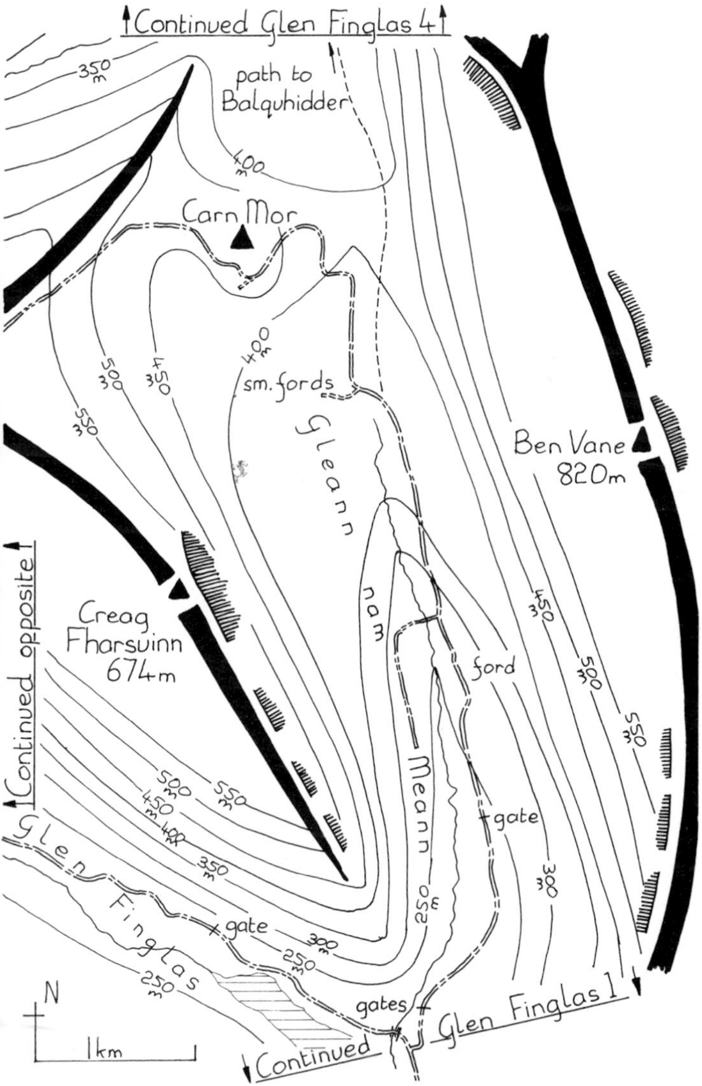

Glen Finglas 4

Although not in the habit of including public roads those shown here are extremely quiet and provide an almost traffic-free connection to Strathyre Forest and Loch Voil. The public road alongside Loch Voil also leads to the River Larig and Monachyle Glen. Further, Glen Ogle should soon be connected by the cycleway. Also, note the hill path to Strathyre village, Ballimore is only 5km or 3miles from the village centre.

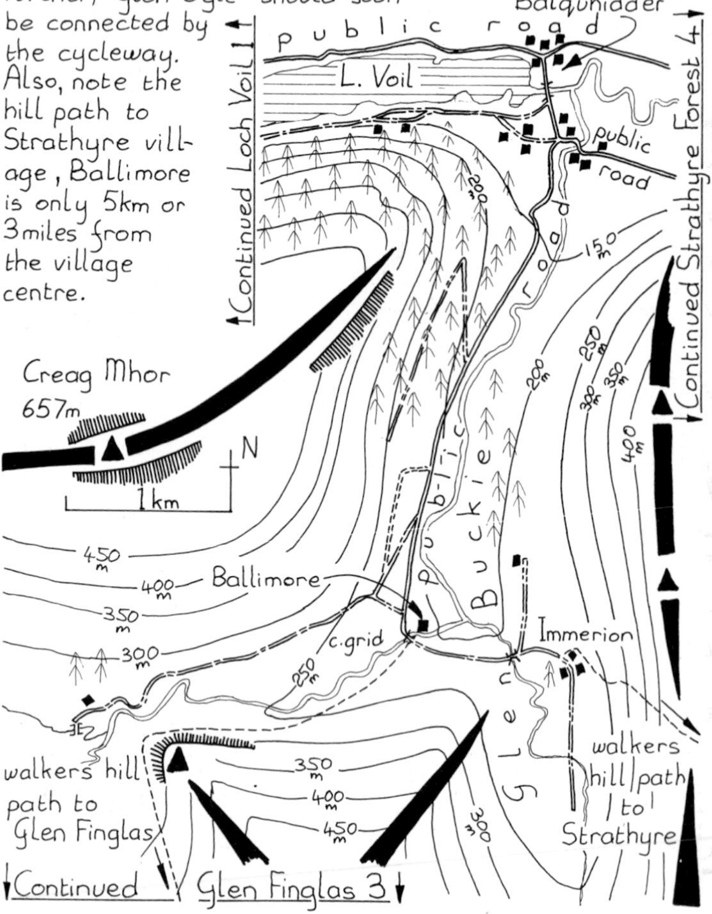

Loch Venachar 1

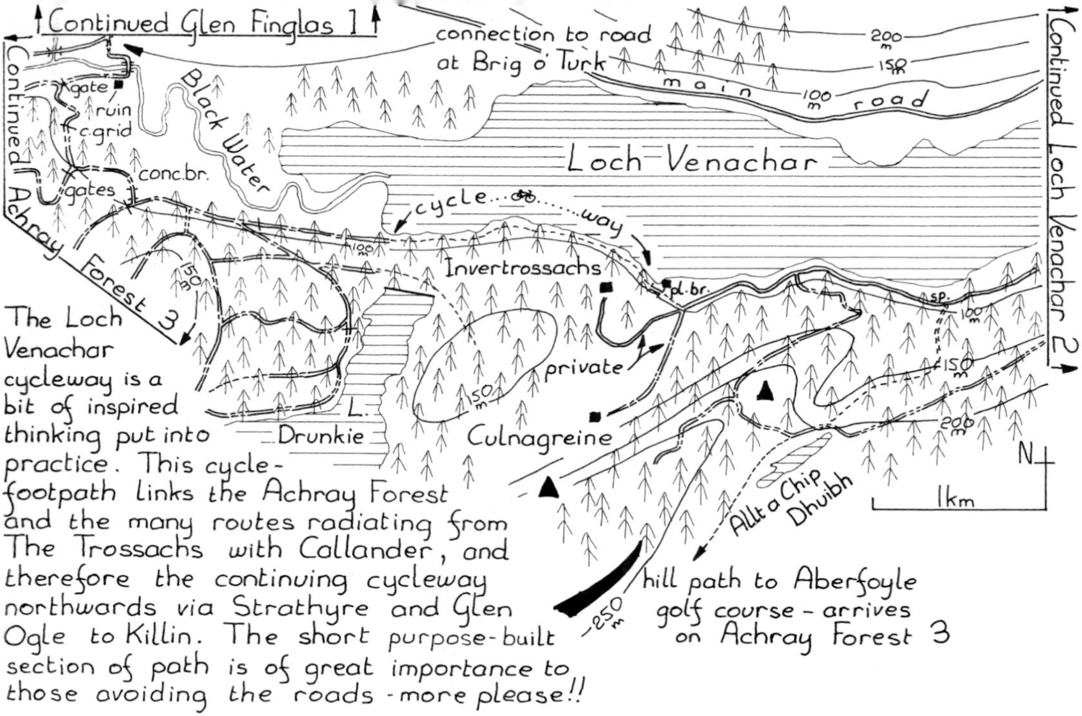

The Loch Venachar cycleway is a bit of inspired thinking put into practice. This cycle-footpath links the Achray Forest and the many routes radiating from The Trossachs with Callander, and therefore the continuing cycleway northwards via Strathyre and Glen Ogle to Killin. The short purpose-built section of path is of great importance to those avoiding the roads - more please!!

Loch Venachar 2

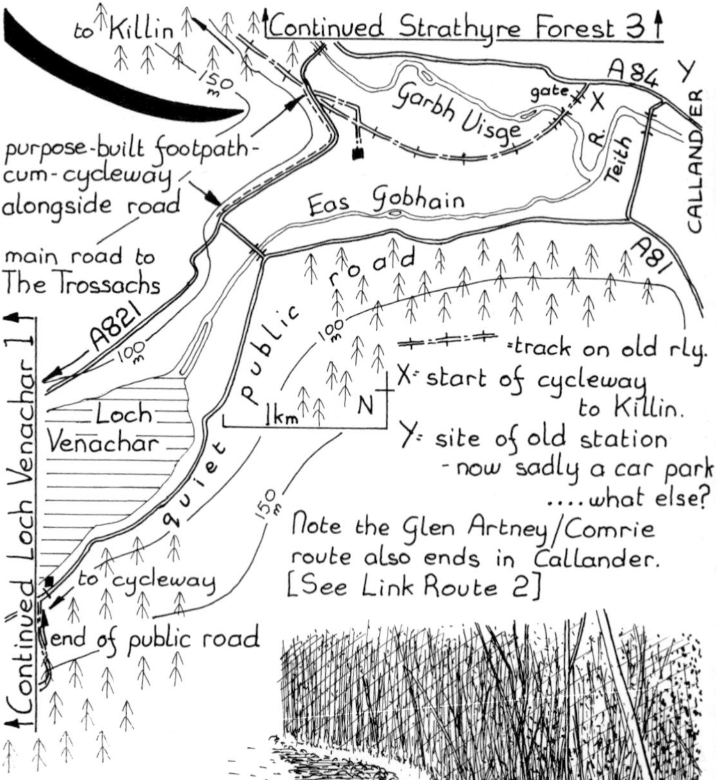

to Killin
Continued Strathyre Forest 3
A84
Y
CALLANDER
gate
X
Garbh Uisge
R. Teith
150 m
purpose-built footpath-cum-cycleway alongside road
Eas Gobhain
main road to The Trossachs
A81
public road
A821
100 m
=track on old rly.
X= start of cycleway to Killin.
Y= site of old station - now sadly a car park ....what else?
Continued Loch Venachar 1
Loch Venachar
1km
N
quiet
150 m
Note the Glen Artney/Comrie route also ends in Callander. [See Link Route 2]
to cycleway
end of public road

Loch Venachar cycleway

Strathyre Forest covers the north-south glen between Balquhidder (for Loch Voil and Glen Ogle), and Callander (for Loch Venachar and Glen Artney). Therefore, besides being a fine route in its own right, it is of some strategic importance in providing the key to some half dozen or more long distance routes. Central to all this is the Glasgow-Killin cycleway which at the time of writing was not quite complete east of Balquhidder. However your hard-working author, knee deep in mud and cow flap, found a way through! Let's hope this section is finalized by the time you arrive in Balquhidder!! The A84 has to be avoided almost at any cost for this is a very busy road and unfortunately one is never far from the noise which emanates from our obsession with the motor car.

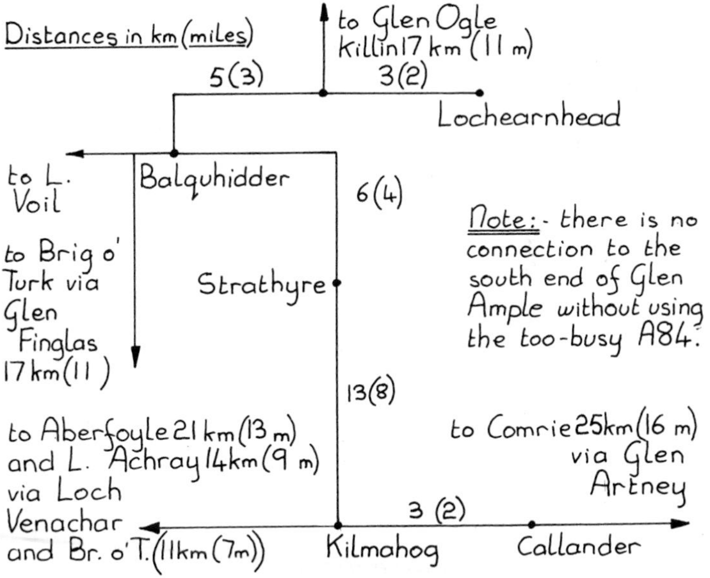

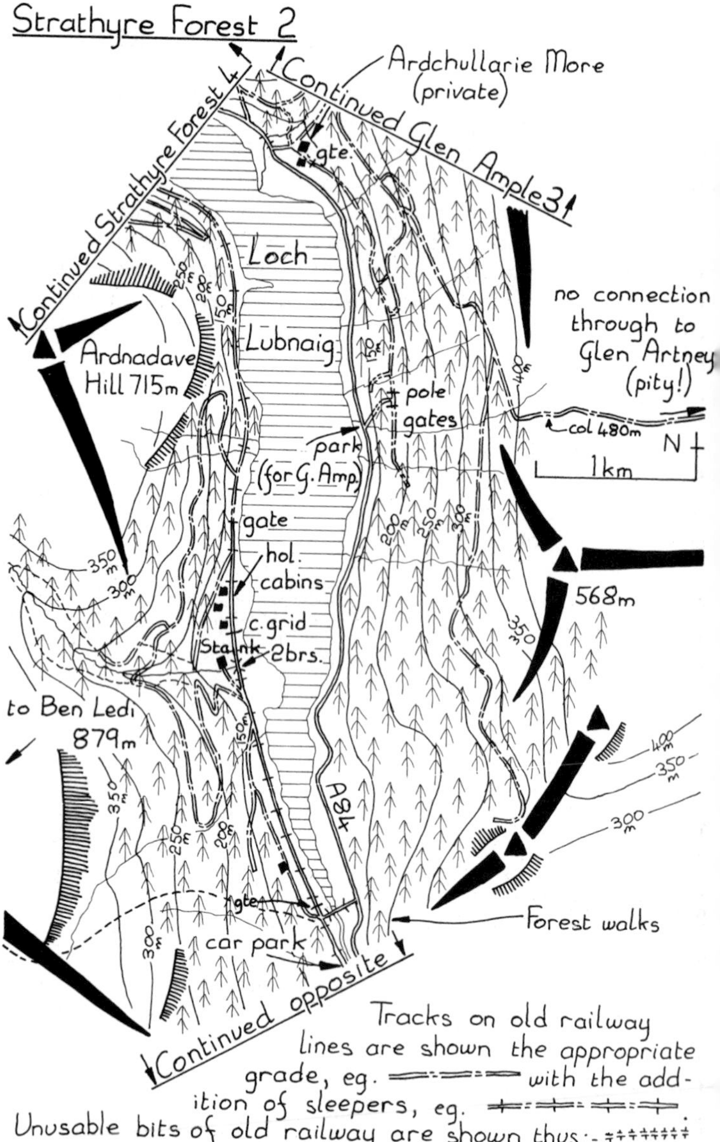
Strathyre Forest 2
Continued Strathyre Forest 4
Continued Glen Ample 3
Ardchullarie More (private)
gte.
Loch
Lubnaig
Ardnadave Hill 715m
no connection through to Glen Artney (pity!)
pole gates
col 480m
N
1km
park (for G. Amp.)
gate
hol. cabins
c. grid
Sta.
tank
2brs.
568m
to Ben Ledi 879m
A84
gte.
car park
Forest walks
Continued opposite
350m
300m
250m
200m
150m
400m
Tracks on old railway lines are shown the appropriate grade, eg. with the addition of sleepers, eg.
Unusable bits of old railway are shown thus:-

Strathyre Forest 3

If one is interested in cycling, walking and railways Strathyre is the place to be. The Callander and Oban railway was built in the 1870s and the Killin branch in 1886. Due to a lack of investment and plain common sense closure of these railways came in 1965. This was not just the closure of a railway but the destruction of part of our infrastructure and our history. Still, the next best thing to an operational railway is a cycleway which retains both infrastructure and history and provides safe, environmentally-friendly enjoyment for walkers and cyclists. At least if people are walking or cycling they are not driving! That has to be better for our health and the environment. So, "on yer bike"!!

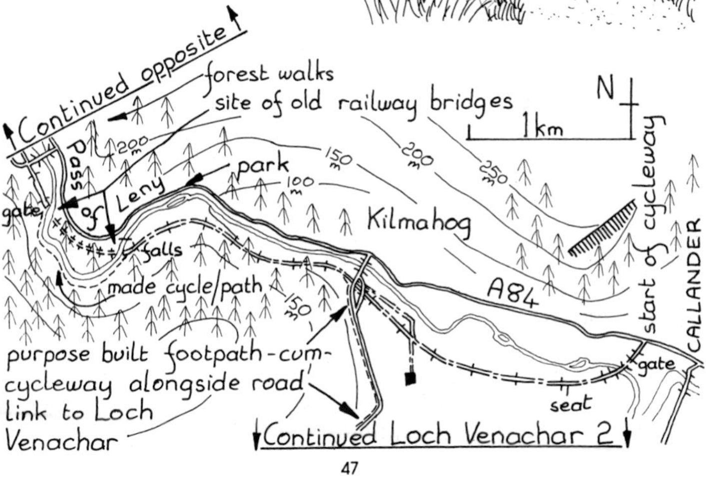

Strathyre Forest 4

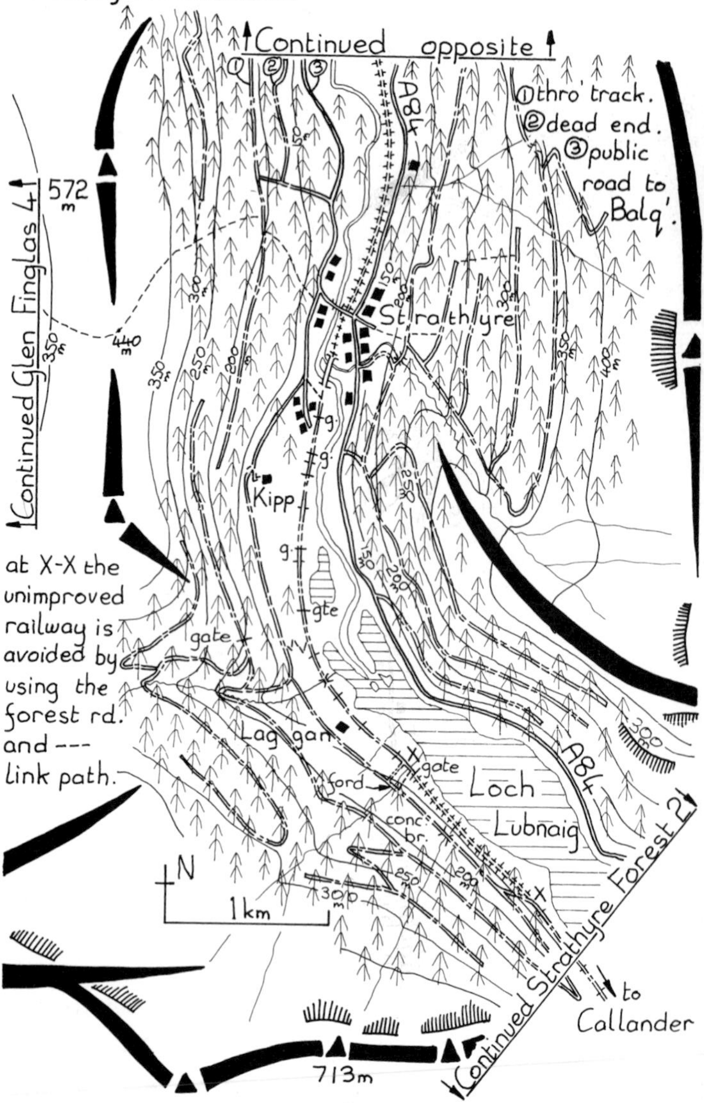
Continued opposite
①thro' track.
②dead end.
③public road to Balq'.
A84
Strathyre
Kipp
Laggan
Loch Lubnaig
572 m
440 m
713m
at X-X the unimproved railway is avoided by using the forest rd. and --- link path.
gate
gte
ford
conc br.
N
1km
to Callander
Continued Glen Finglas 4
Continued Strathyre Forest 2

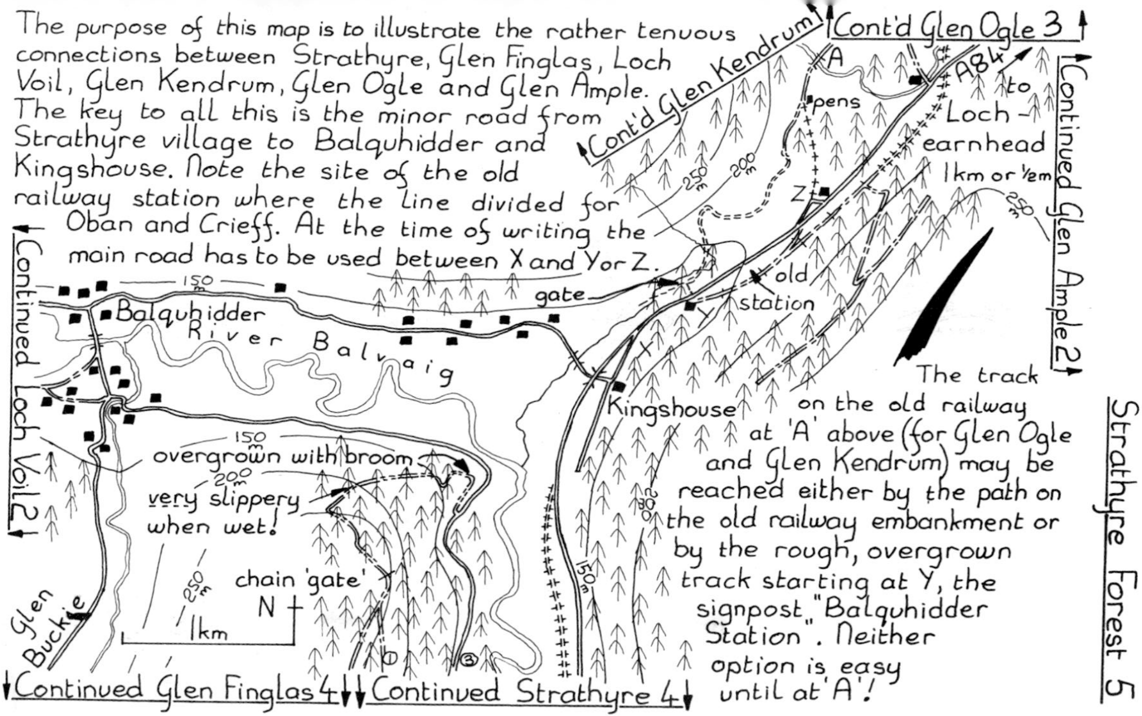
Strathyre Forest 5
The purpose of this map is to illustrate the rather tenuous connections between Strathyre, Glen Finglas, Loch Voil, Glen Kendrum, Glen Ogle and Glen Ample. The key to all this is the minor road from Strathyre village to Balquhidder and Kingshouse. Note the site of the old railway station where the line divided for Oban and Crieff. At the time of writing the main road has to be used between X and Y or Z.
Cont'd Glen Kendrum
Cont'd Glen Ogle 3
Continued Glen Ample 2
A
A84
to Loch-earnhead
pens
Z
1km or ½m
250m
200m
150m
gate
old station
Y
Balquhidder
River Balvaig
Kingshouse
The track on the old railway at 'A' above (for Glen Ogle and Glen Kendrum) may be reached either by the path on the old railway embankment or by the rough, overgrown track starting at Y, the signpost "Balquhidder Station". Neither option is easy until at 'A'!
overgrown with broom
very slippery when wet!
chain 'gate'
N
1km
Glen Buckie
Continued Loch Voil 2
Continued Glen Finglas 4
Continued Strathyre 4

South Tayside and Lochearnhead

South Tayside and Lochearnhead

Access:- My arbitrary South Tayside and Lochearnhead region covers the area south of Glen Dochart and Loch Tay centred around Glen Ogle and Lochearnhead. Access is via the A84 and A85 which are very busy trunk roads, the former approaching from Callander in the south and the latter passing from west to east via Glen Dochart and Loch Earn. The heavy traffic on these roads detracts from the peace of the region.

Accommodation:- The main centres are Killin and Lochearnhead, with Kenmore in the north east of the area. Killin has tourist information (April to September), hotels, B&Bs, caravan and camping sites and an SYHA hostel. This is the best centre, off the main trunk roads but still very busy in the summer. (Dochart Bridge seems to have a coach party permanently glued to it all summer, blissfully unaware of its main road status!). Lochearnhead has less to offer, whilst Kenmore is the main boating centre for Loch Tay - also busy in summer.

Geographical Features:- Many of the routes lie on forest track or railway, Glen Ample providing a welcome change. The narrow Glen Ogle contrasts with the open strath of Glen Dochart. An area of rounded hills, the undramatic mountain scenery is compensated by interest in the glens. Evidence of the ice age is shown by the hanging valley of Ardtalnaig Glen where the side-glen drops steeply to the main glen (Loch Tay).

Mountains:- Bleak grouse moor, deep in heather occupies much of the high ground, culminating in unexciting rounded hills at about 600-800m high. The absence of respectable mountains is relieved by views of Ben Lawers to the north of Loch Tay. Even Ben Chonzie really belongs to the next section, being between Glen Almond and Glen Lednock, but deserving mention here as access may be gained from Ardtalnaig Glen as a diversion on the way through to Glen Lednock.

Rivers:- The Ardchyle Burn in Gleann Dubh, Lochan Breaclaich and the Artalnaig Burn drain into the Tay. Actually the Ardchyle Burn drains into the River Dochart which only becomes the Tay at the other end of the loch. Similarly the Ogle Burn and Kendrum Burn become the River Earn upon leaving Loch Earn. The Ample Burn joins them in the loch. The River Larig picks up the Monachyle Burn and becomes the River Balvag on its way down Strathyre to the River Teith.

Forests:- The main area of planted forest is to the south of Killin, swallowing up the old railway, but more open higher tracks provide extensive views. Loch Voil and Monachyle Glen owe their tracks to the forest as does the southern end of the Glen Ample route. Natural woods are limited to pockets of birch in sheltered areas, the best of which are along the southern shore of Loch Tay.

Lochs :- The star of the show is Loch Tay, best appreciated from the saddle of a bicycle along the quiet south shore, similarly Loch Earn. Loch Voil may be enjoyed either along the Loch Voil forest tracks or the quiet public road. Lochan Breaclaich is a bleak stretch of water complete with a dam and a disused quarry used in its construction. A man made intrusion in an area of otherwise natural lochs, at their proper levels.

Emergency :- There is little opportunity to become stranded in this area. Note the Gleann Dubh/Glen Kendrum col is high (yours truly did this in a snow storm!) and Ardtalnaig Glen/Glen Lednock is a committing walk not to be underestimated, again with a high watershed. Other routes are short with civilization (unfortunately) near at hand.

South Tayside and Lochearnhead Routes 1

River Larig

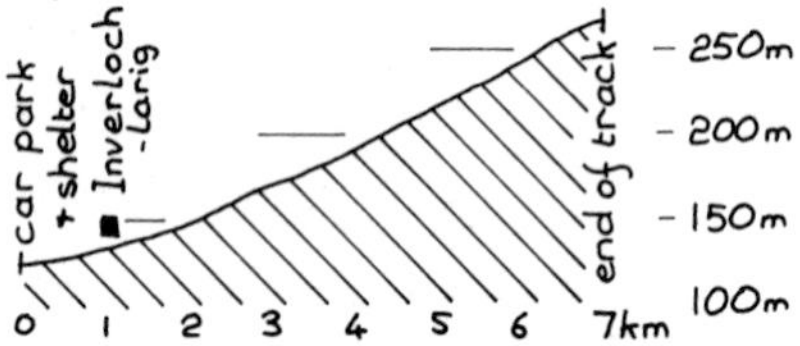

Loch Voil

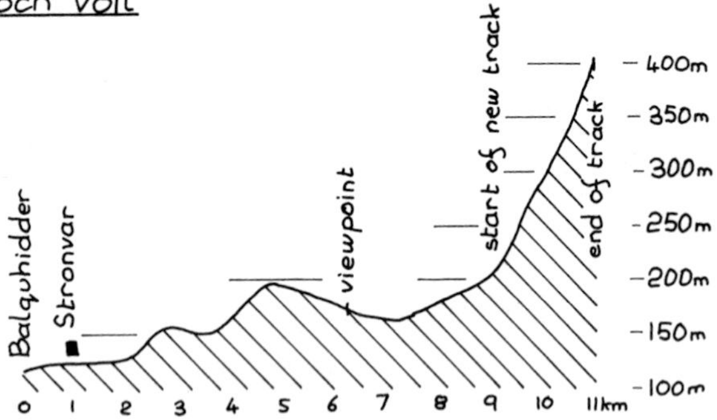

Monachyle Glen

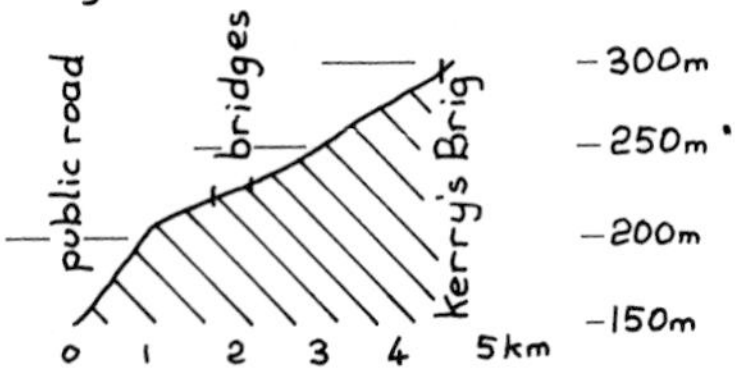

South Tayside and Lochearnhead Routes 2

Gleann Dubh/Glen Kendrum

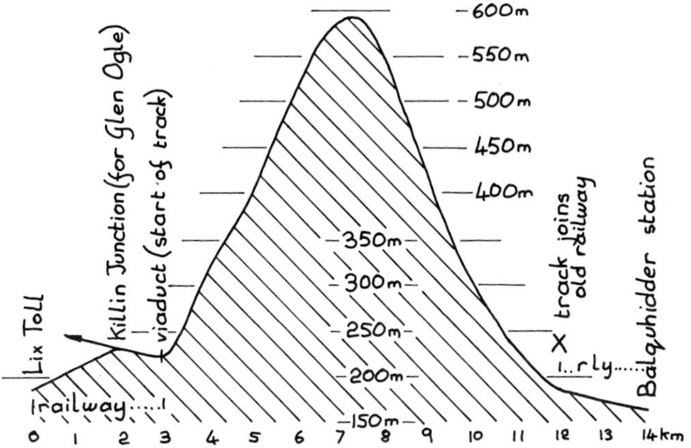

Glen Ogle (from Killin)

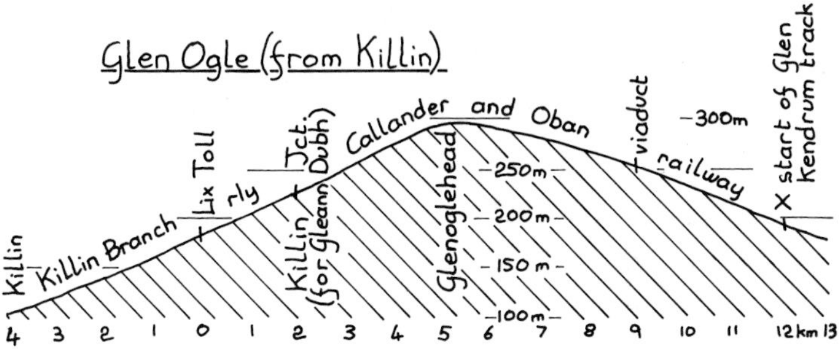

Glen Ample

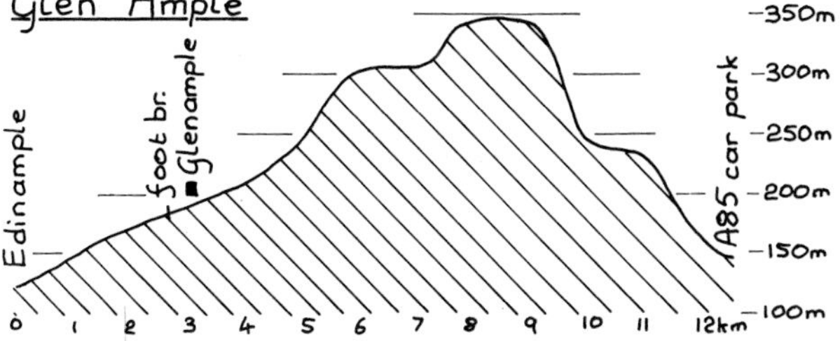

South Tayside and Lochearnhead Routes 3

Lochan Breaclaich

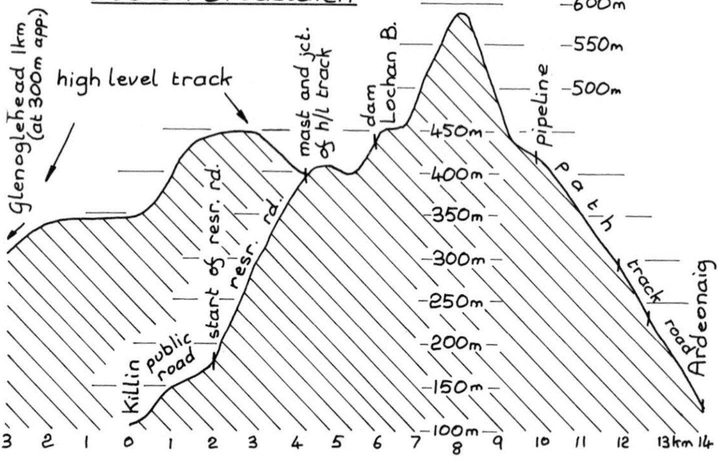

Ardtalnaig Glen

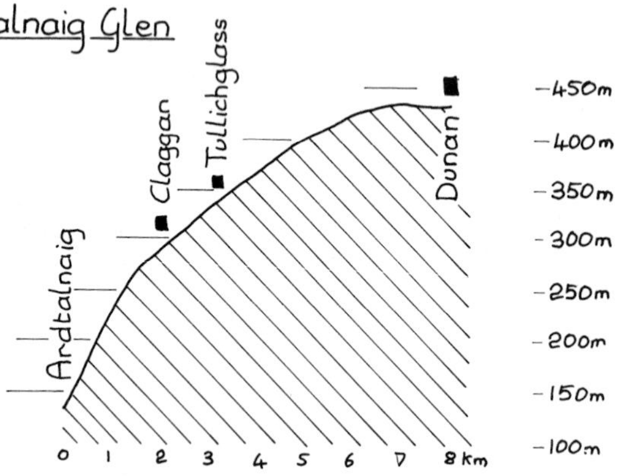

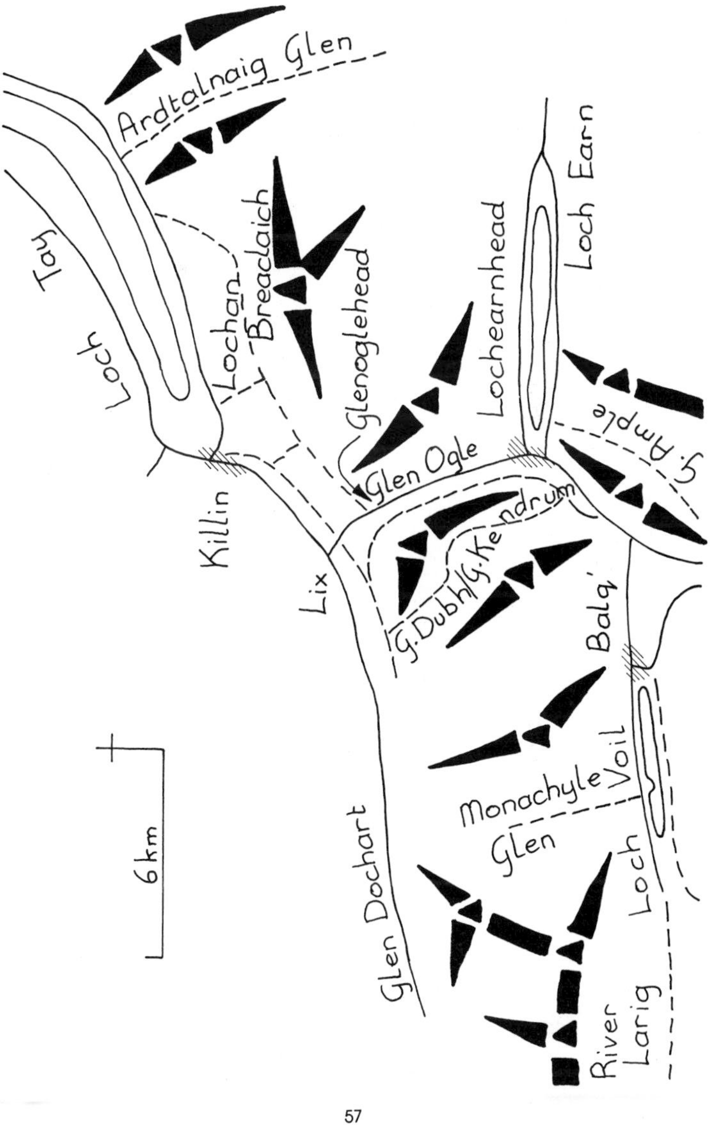

Ardtalnaig Glen
Loch Tay
Lochan Breaclaich
Glenoglehead
Lochearnhead
Loch Earn
Glen Ogle
G. Ample
Killin
G. Kendrum
G. Dubh
Lix
Balq.
Monachyle
Voil
Glen
Loch
Glen Dochart
River Larig
6km

River Larig 1

The River Larig is a short out-and-back cycle ride or may be used as the starting point for a more adventurous walk to Crianlarich or Loch Katrine by the paths indicated on the information board at the start. The indistinct continuing path links up with Glen Gyle and Loch Katrine and the West Highland Way in Glen Falloch. I was politely asked by the landowner for £1 for taking a bike up the track. This is fair enough in my view. (I can almost hear the howls of protest!). After all, this is private land, and the landowner's reasons for the charge, maintenance of the track and keeping an eye on who is where, seem reasonable, and more positive than a ban on bikes as seen elsewhere.

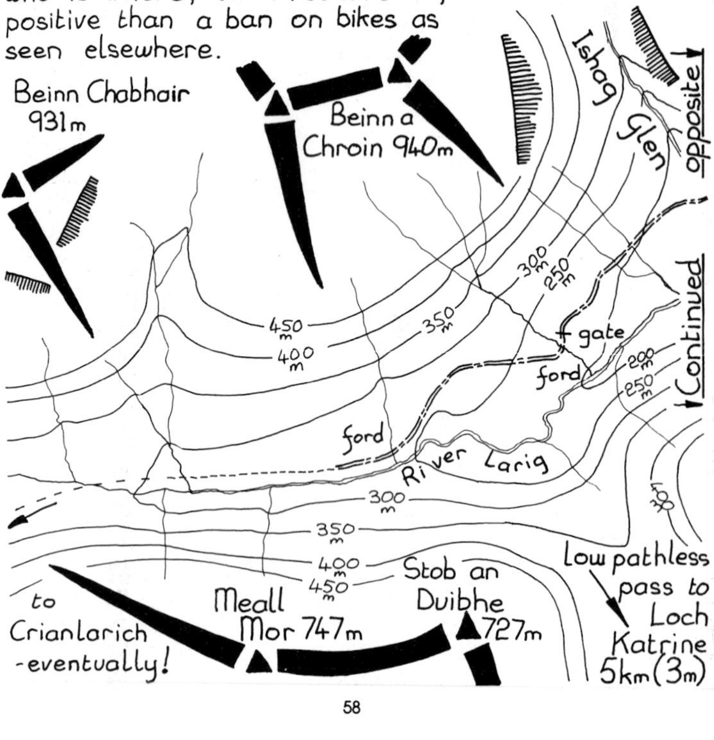

River Larig 2

The Crianlarich hills to the north west are a magnificent collection of 'Munros'; serious mountains for serious hill-walkers.

tourist info.

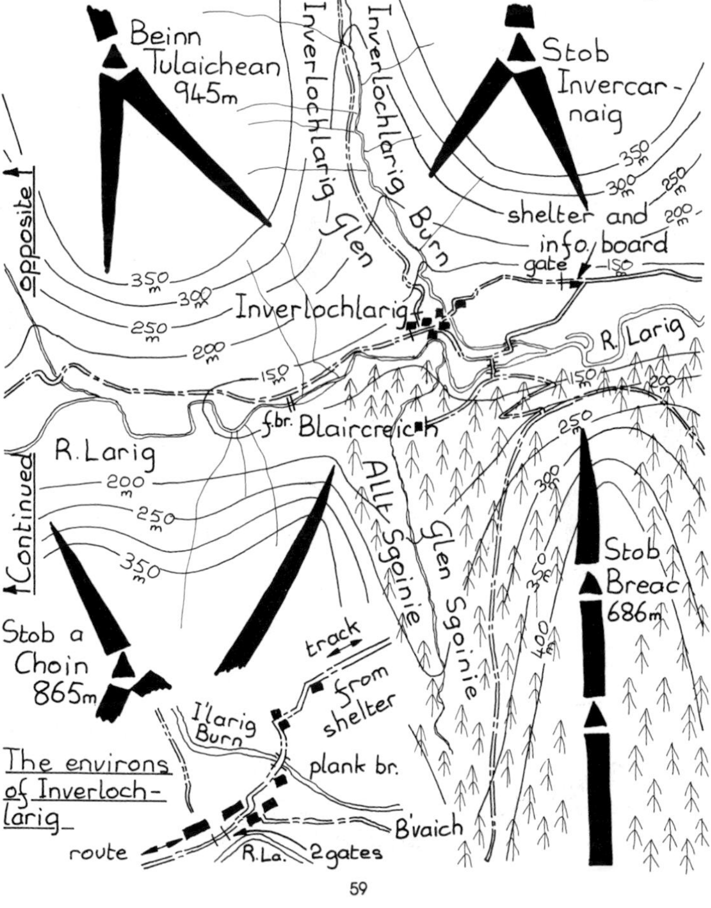

The environs of Inverlochlarig

Loch Voil 1

The Loch Voil track traverses the hills to the south of the loch. The track is high enough to give good views over the loch and beyond, and ends with a new section rising to a dead-end which may or may not be worth exploring, depending upon one's energy levels! There is no connection, off-road, with the River Larig tracks, the nearest of which restricts the use of cycles anyway. (The public road on the north side of the Loch is quiet enough to provide a safe connection of both routes). The end of the track is 11 km (7 m) from Balquhidder.

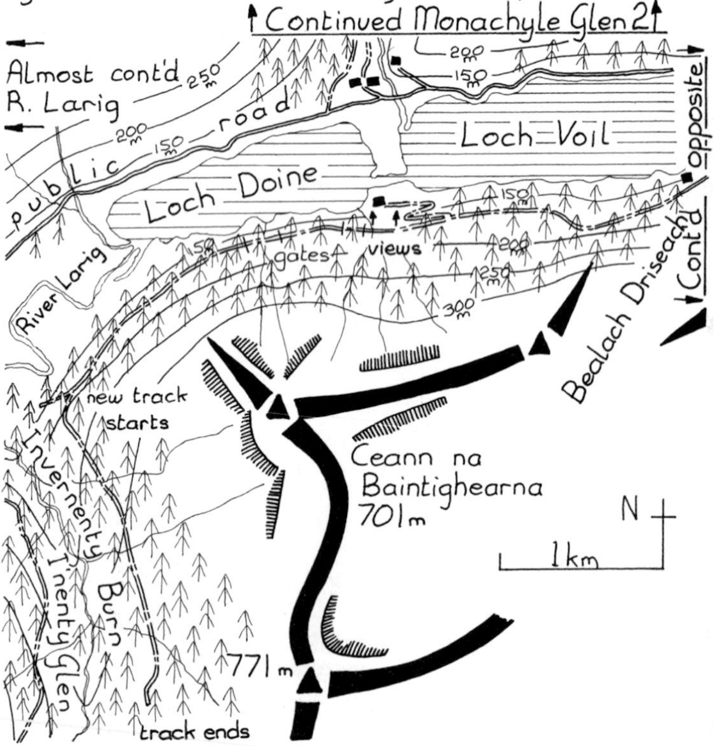

Loch Voil 2

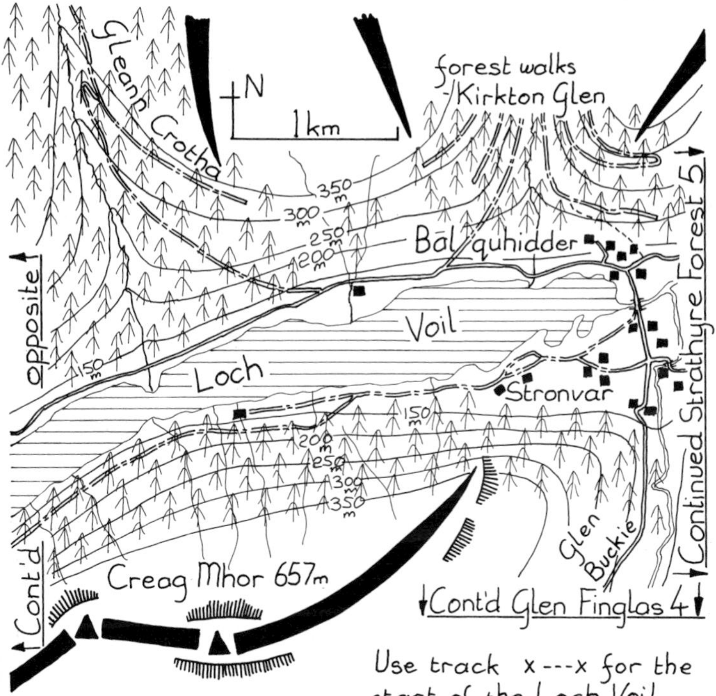

Use track x---x for the start of the Loch Voil lochside track.

Monachyle Glen 1

Monachyle Glen is a walk. The route starts with a locked gate and a high stile and the Forestry Commission have not seen fit to encourage cycling here. The track is short and probably would not be worth the trip by bike. On the day yours truly surveyed this area the weather was so bad I wouldn't have taken my bike out in it anyway. Neither can I comment on the views - except that up to 50 metres all you can see is trees - and Kerry's Brig, beyond which the lads from the Hydrology Dept. were measuring the rainfall - very appropriate! More planting is planned higher up the glen, complete with a bit more track. The walk at present (one way) is only 4·5 km or 3 miles. Sorry for being so negative, but it was so wet....!! To the north west Monachyle Glen provides access to some interesting ridges culminating in Ben More at 1174 metres.

Kerry's Brig

Monachyle Glen 2

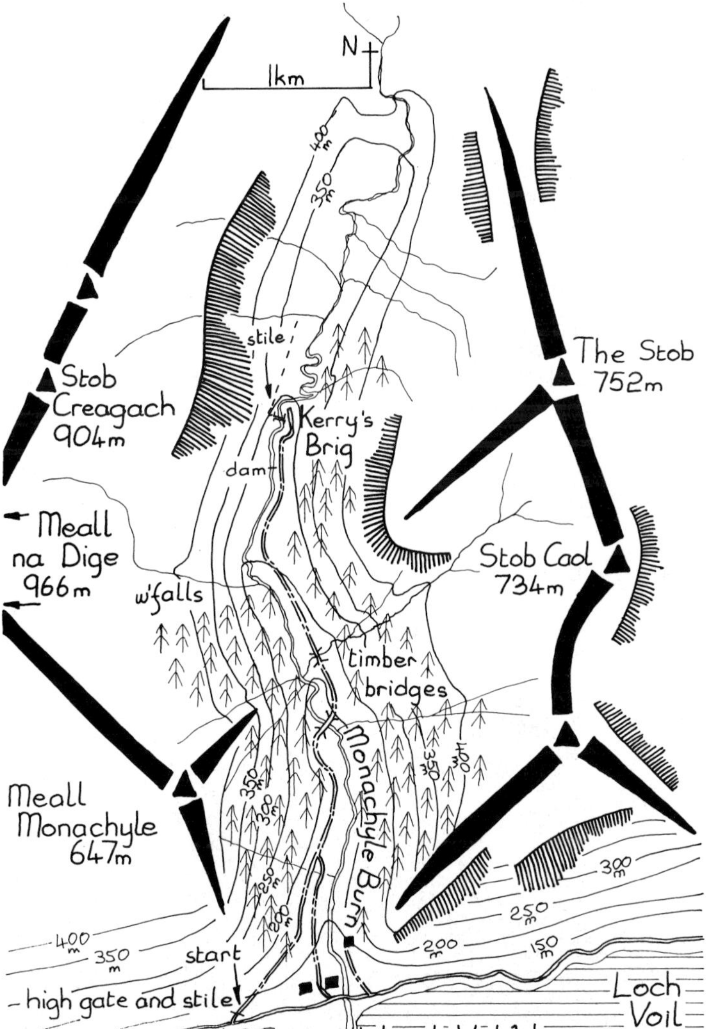

Continued Loch Voil 1

Gleann Dubh/Glen Kendrum 1

Gleann Dubh and Glen Kendrum have been put into one section as both are short, yet together provide a good through route from Glen Dochart to Lochearnhead. Parallel to Glen Ogle this makes a 20km (13m) round trip from Glenoglehead. The start/finish point for the circuit is best from Glenoglehead or Killin as this avoids the road connection at Lochearnhead which is, at the time of writing, difficult with a bike. (See comment Strathyre Forest 5). For walkers there is a direct, steep, path from the Glen Ogle railway to Lochearnhead. Study of this section, Glen Ogle and Loch Breaclaich, will reveal many possible circular bike rides or longer walks. The Gleann Dubh/Glen Kendrum watershed is high at 600m (nearly 2000ft). The station at Killin Junction is of interest - a large interchange station complete with three platforms, station buildings, cottages, two signalboxes and no road to it! Here passengers on the Callander and Oban railway changed for Killin.

Ghost train-Gleann Dubh

Gleann Dubh/Glen Kendrum 2

The steep track across Glen Dochart is "Auchlyn West Burn", see Book 3 The Glens of Rannoch.

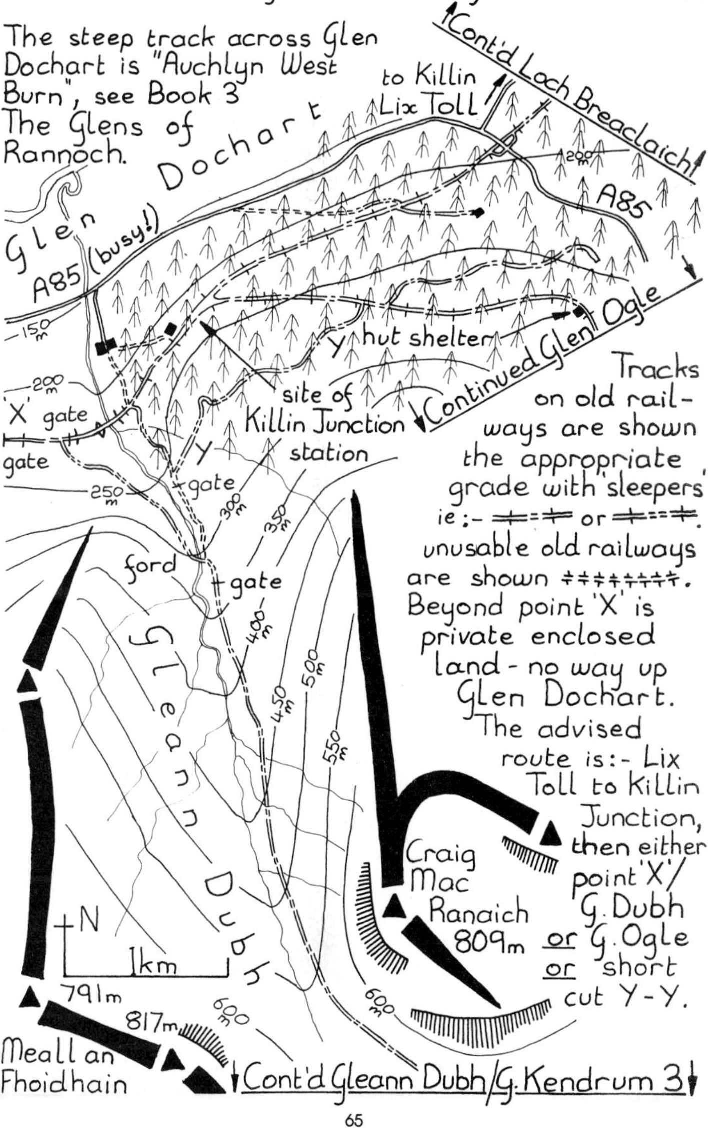

Tracks on old railways are shown the appropriate grade with 'sleepers' ie:- ═╪═╪═ or ═╪═╪═. unusable old railways are shown ╪╪╪╪╪╪╪╪. Beyond point 'X' is private enclosed land - no way up Glen Dochart. The advised route is:- Lix Toll to Killin Junction, then either point 'X'/G. Dubh or G. Ogle or short cut Y-Y.

Gleann Dubh/Glen Kendrum 3

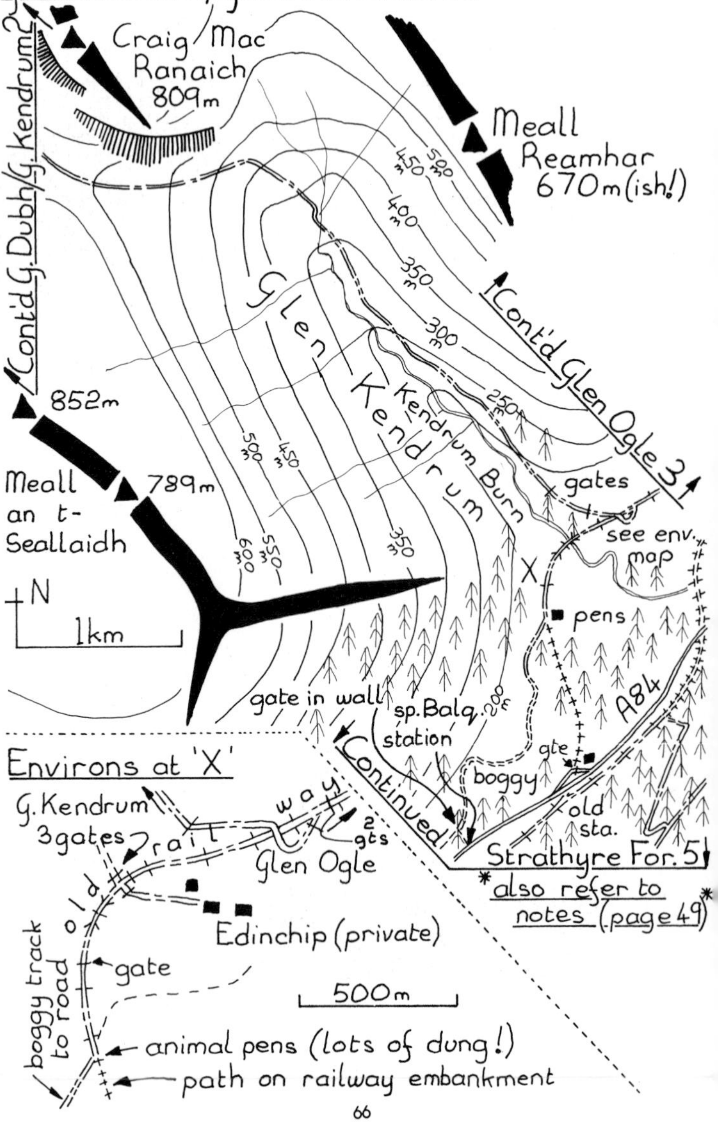
Cont'd G. Dubh/G. Kendrum 2
Craig Mac Ranaich 809m
Meall Reamhar 670m (ish!)
500m
450m
400m
350m
300m
250m
Cont'd Glen Ogle 3
Glen Kendrum
Kendrum Burn
852m
Meall an t-Seallaidh
789m
500m
450m
600m
550m
350m
200m
N
1km
gates
see env. map
X
pens
A84
gate in wall
sp. Balq. station
Continued
gte
boggy
old sta.
Strathyre For. 5
* also refer to notes (page 49) *
Environs at 'X'
G. Kendrum 3 gates
rail way
2 gts
Glen Ogle
old road
Edinchip (private)
gate
boggy track to road
500m
animal pens (lots of dung!)
path on railway embankment

Glen Ogle 1

The route up Glen Ogle forms the main link between Strathyre Forest and Killin. In addition to circular walks or bike rides via Gleann Dubh and Glen Kendrum, alternatives exist within Glen Ogle using two versions of the old road or a nature trail (for walkers only) for the return. Glen Ogle, by its narrow form, has compressed the transport "corridor" into a width of 500m providing a view of our changing modes of transport. One abandoned railway and two abandoned roads give way to the noisy, polluting A85 which is all too evident in the glen. What next? Will the main road be abandoned for a motorway or some super-highway? The answer is to move information, not people. People should move around on trains and bikes. This cycle-way is an admirable start! Balquhidder station to Lix Toll via Killin Junction is 14km (9m) – or to Glenoglehead (for Loch Breaclaich) is 9km (6m). Both lead on to Killin.

The platelayer's hut

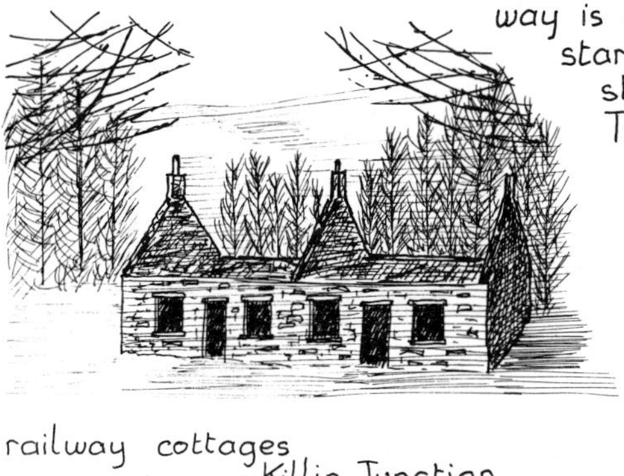

railway cottages – Killin Junction

Glen Ogle 2

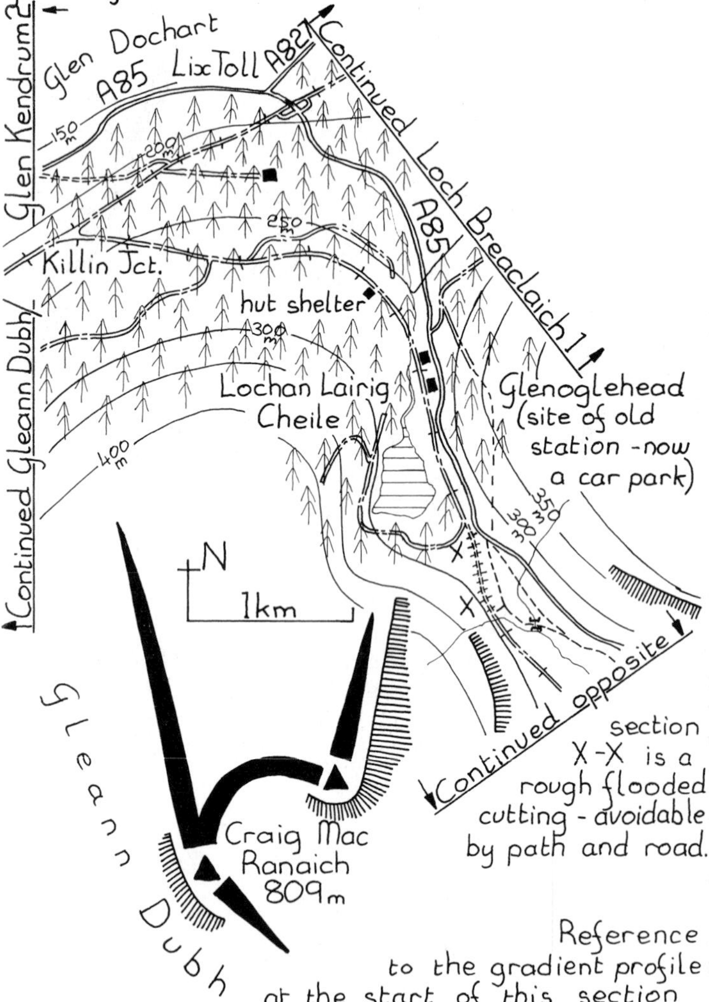

section X-X is a rough flooded cutting - avoidable by path and road.

Reference to the gradient profile at the start of this section will reveal that despite the railway, Glen Ogle is anything but flat. The climb up to Glenoglehead from both north and south is considerable.

Glen Ogle 3

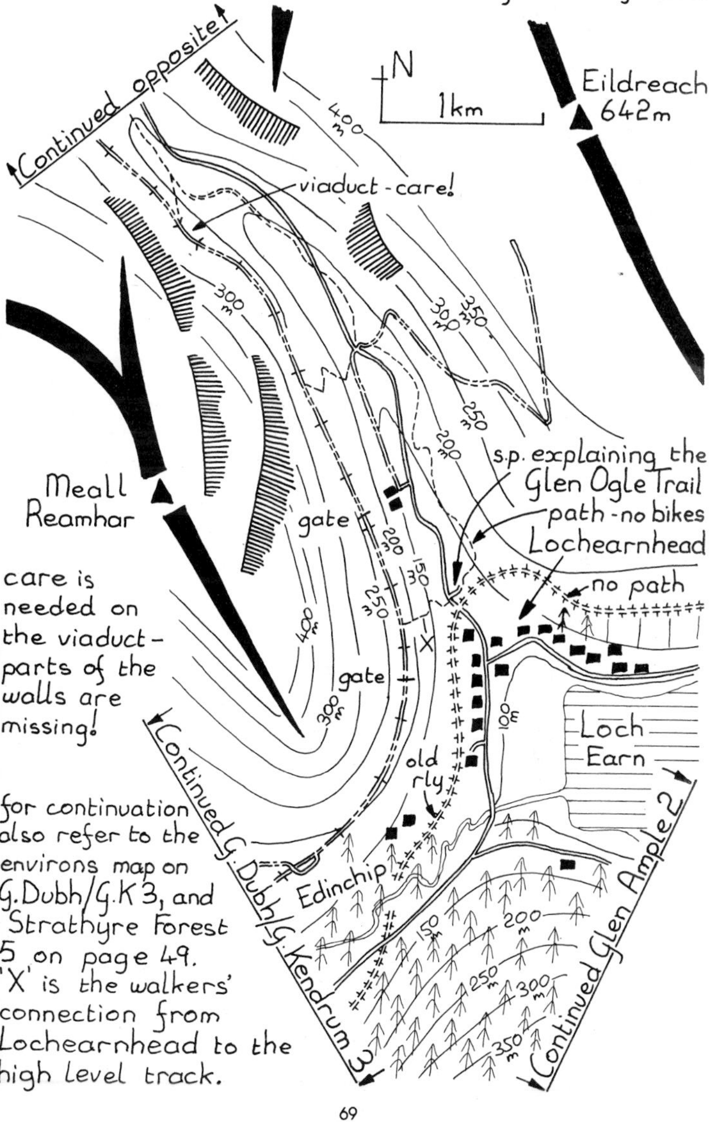

care is needed on the viaduct - parts of the walls are missing!

for continuation also refer to the environs map on G.Dubh/G.K 3, and Strathyre Forest 5 on page 49.
'X' is the walkers' connection from Lochearnhead to the high level track.

Lochan Breaclaich 1

The high tracks above Killin and its railway not only lead up to the dam and Lochan Breaclaich but provide off road links to the railway trail in Glen Ogle, and the track up Gleann Dubh, by using the old Killin branch line via Lix Toll and Killin Junction. Alternatively a direct track leads to Glenoglehead (better in descent on a bike) See environs map opposite for start from Killin.

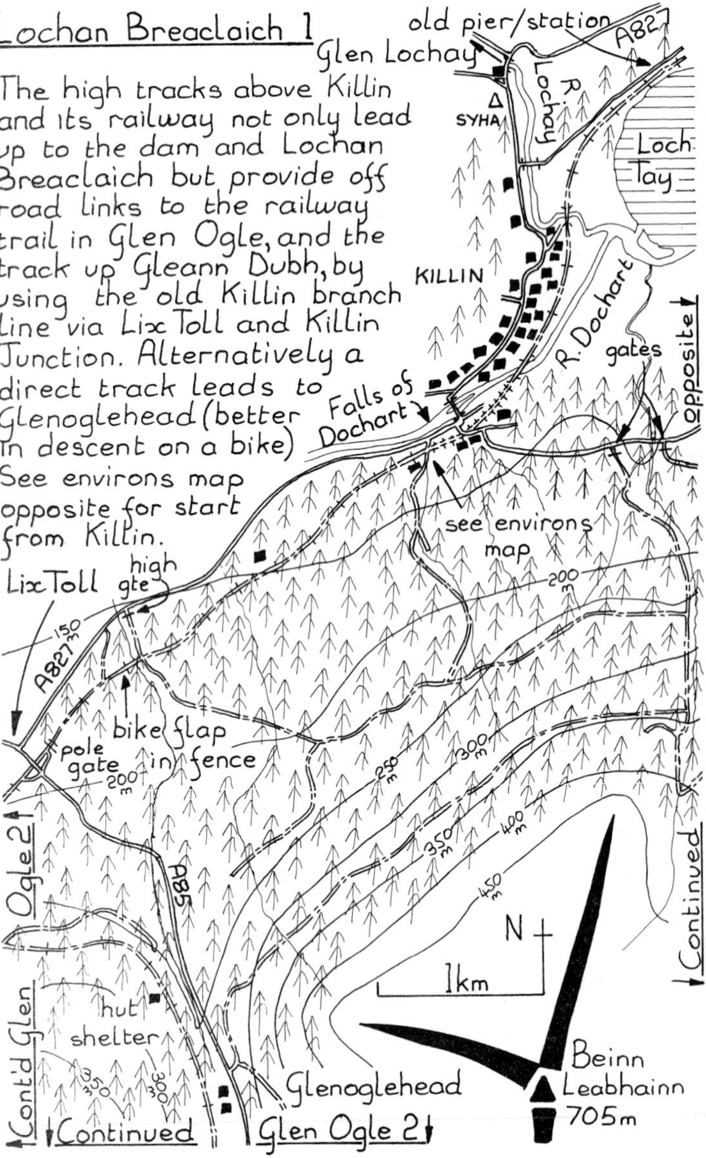

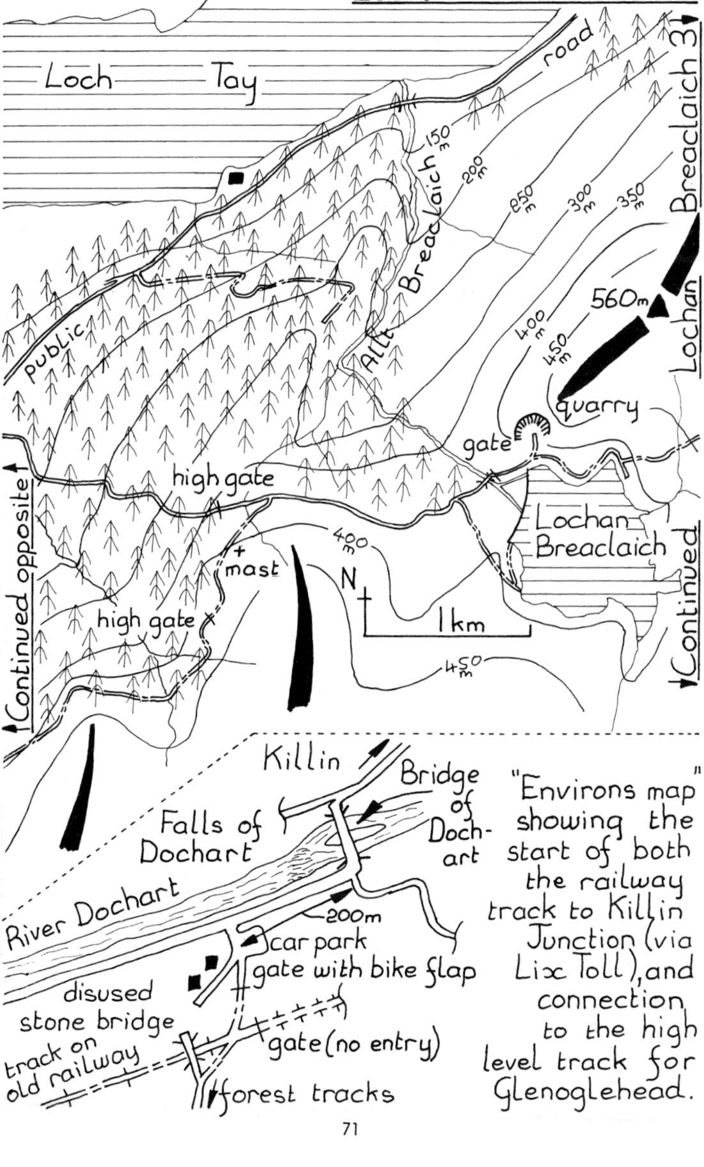

Lochan Breaclaich 2
Loch Tay
road
public
Allt Breaclaich
150 m
200 m
250 m
300 m
350 m
400 m
450 m
560m
Lochan Breaclaich 3
quarry
gate
high gate
Lochan Breaclaich
Continued opposite
Continued
mast
N
1km
high gate
400 m
450 m
Killin
Bridge of Doch-art
Falls of Dochart
River Dochart
200m
car park
gate with bike flap
disused stone bridge
track on old railway
gate (no entry)
forest tracks
"Environs map" showing the start of both the railway track to Killin Junction (via Lix Toll), and connection to the high level track for Glenoglehead.

Lochan Breaclaich 3

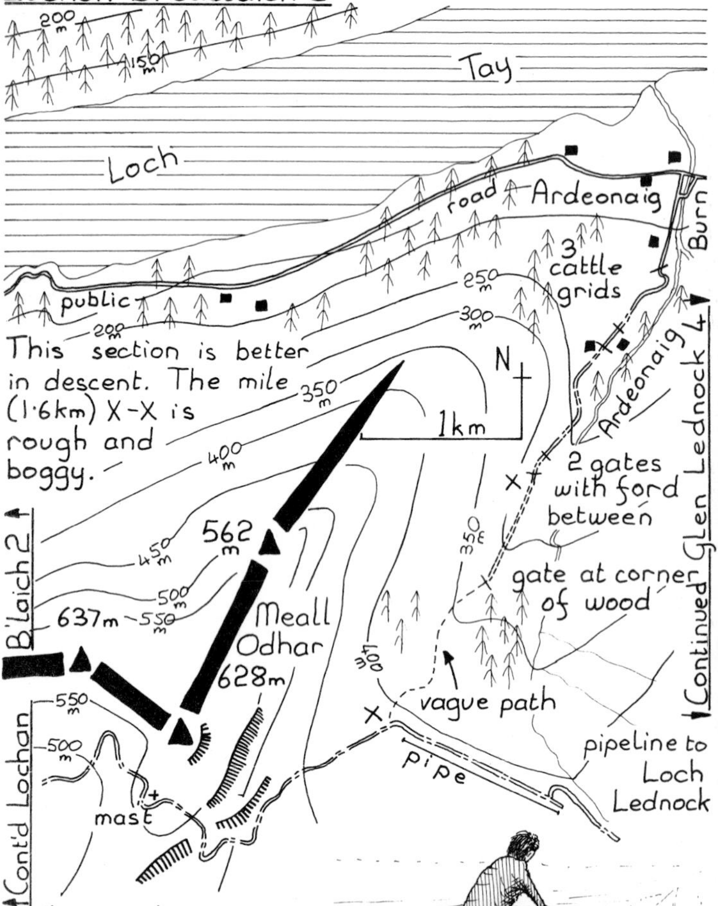

cycling in the snow above Killin

Glen Ample 1

Glen Ample provides an excellent link from Lochearnhead to Strathyre, an interesting walk, yet not too rough to cycle. The only snag is that at the southern end the track ends at the side of the busy A85. So, unless one arrives with transport arranged (or at 5am on Sunday) the two miles or so to the bridge leading to the Strathyre Forest cycleway is fraught with the danger of passing traffic. As a walk, from the start of Glen Ample to the A85 car park is 12km (8miles). As a bike ride (including running the gauntlet on the main road) the round trip from Lochearnhead via Glen Ample, the Pass of Leny and Strathyre Forest is 39km (24m); from Callander the Strathyre/Glen Ample circuit is 43km (30m). Both suggestions include the minor road loop to Balquhidder. There is no shelter in Glen Ample. There are fine views both north and south, as below, from the watershed. The route provides a change from the many forest tracks in the region.

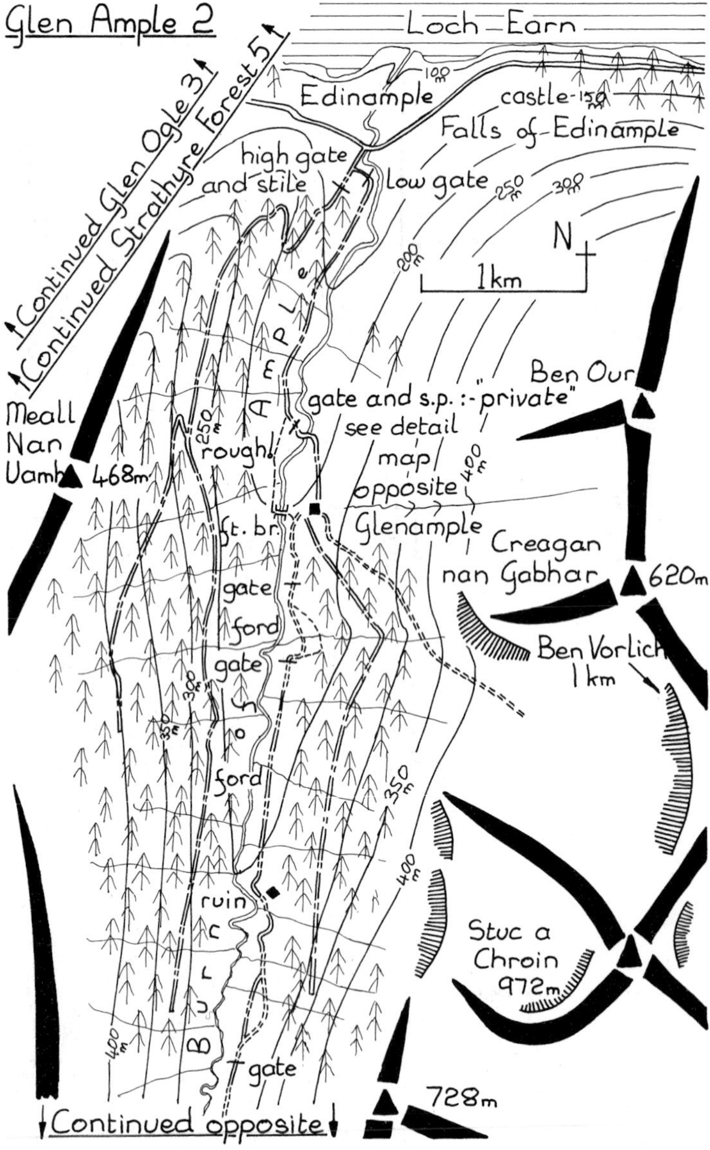
Glen Ample 2
Loch Earn
Continued Glen Ogle 3
Continued Strathyre Forest 5
100m
Edinample
castle
150m
Falls of Edinample
high gate and stile
low gate
250m
300m
200m
N
1km
AMPLE
Ben Our
Meall Nan Uamh
468m
250m
rough
gate and s.p. :- "private"
see detail map opposite
400m
ft. br.
Glenample
Creagan nan Gabhar
620m
gate
ford
gate
Ben Vorlich 1km
300m
350m
ford
350m
400m
ruin
Stuc a Chroin 972m
400m
BUCL
gate
728m
Continued opposite

Glen Ample 3

The environs of Glenample

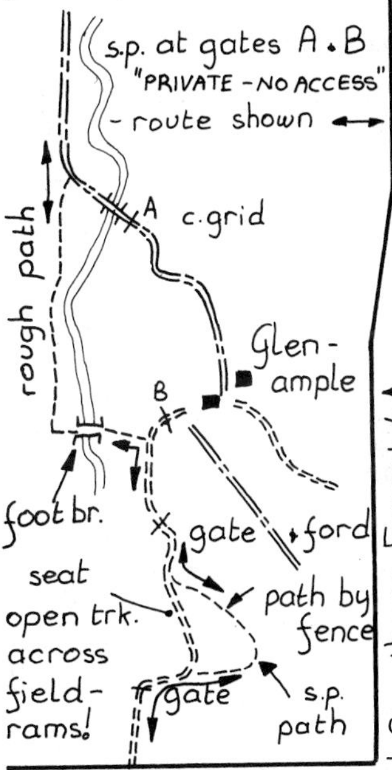

Forest track 'X' runs to a dead end just off this map - no connection through to Glen Artney.

Note:-

Strathyre Forest 2 also depicts the link to the Strathyre cycleway via the bridge at the Pass of Leny.

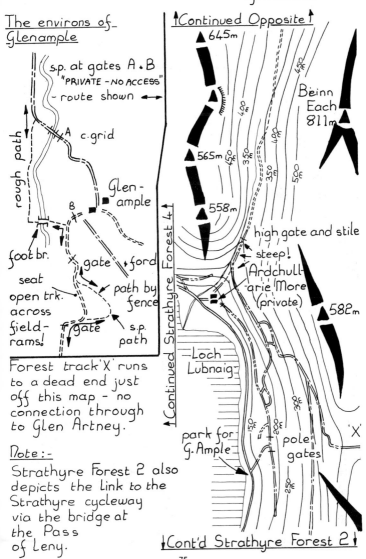

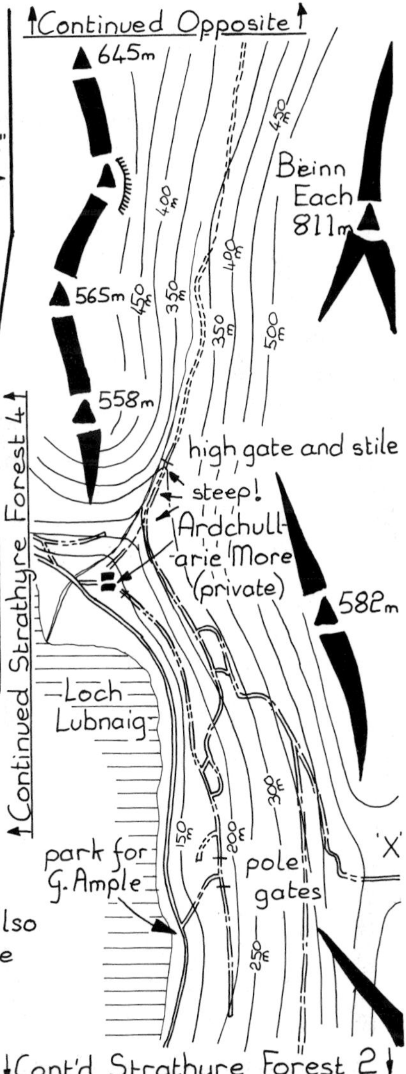

Ardtalnaig Glen 1 (or Gleann a Chilleine)

Ardtalnaig Glen forms the north western end of an excellent through route from Glen Almond with a branch path to Glen Lednock. The track rises from the farms of Ardtalnaig Glen and soon passes into the wilds of Gleann a Chilleine, following a good track all the way to Dunan. About a mile of footpath makes the link into Glen Almond at which point the alternative walkers' link branches off to Glen Lednock via the north western shoulder of Ben Chonzie. The branch tracks are used for stalking and shooting the long-suffering grouse. Apart from the Glen Lednock path our route stays at the bottom of the glen rising to 440m at Dunan or 633m by Ben Chonzie. Dunan provides emergency shelter and there are no major fords. Ardtalnaig to Dunan is 8km (4·5m); to the public road in Glen Almond is 24 km (15 m) Ardtalnaig to Invergeldie in Glen Lednock is 17 km (10m).

Dunan

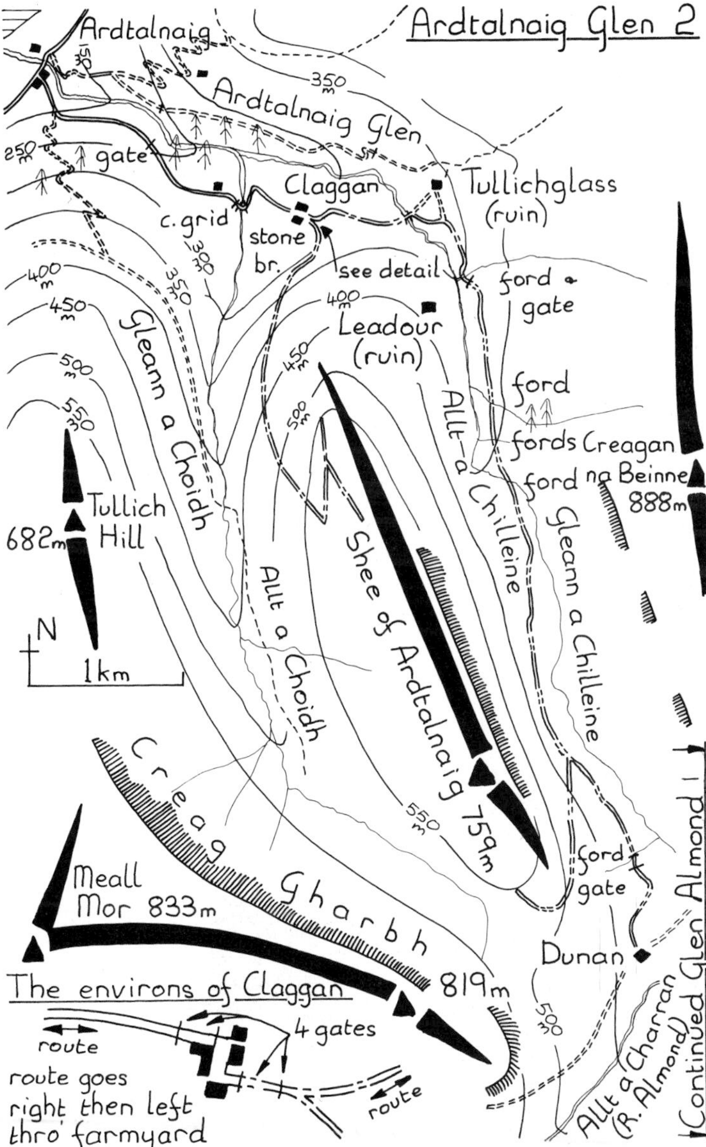
Ardtalnaig Glen 2
Ardtalnaig
Ardtalnaig Glen
350 m
250 m
150 m
gate
Claggan
Tullichglass (ruin)
c. grid
stone br.
see detail
300 m
350 m
400 m
450 m
500 m
550 m
ford
gate
Leadour (ruin)
ford
fords
Creagan na Beinne 888m
ford
Gleann a Choidh
Allt a Chilleine
Gleann a Chilleine
Allt a Choidh
Shee of Ardtalnaig 759m
Tullich Hill 682m
N
1km
Creag Gharbh 819m
Meall Mor 833m
ford
gate
Dunan
Continued Glen Almond
Allt a Charran (R. Almond)
The environs of Claggan
4 gates
route
route goes right then left thro' farmyard
route

Callander
to
Comrie

Callander to Comrie

Access:- This region is centred around Glen Artney, which, running from near Callander to Comrie, provides the main link for the other glens. Road access is from the A84 Callander to Lochearnhead or A87 Lochearnhead to Comrie roads, linked northwards by Glen Ogle, east by Crieff and south by Doune and Dunblane. The nearest railway stations are Gleneagles or Perth.
Accommodation:- Although Callander, Lochearnhead and Comrie are the main centres the only tourist information in the area is the Rob Roy and Trossachs visitor centre in Callander (Mar-Dec). The tourist info centre at Crieff is open all year. The Comrie to Crieff area has a wide variety of accommodation with caravanners and campers well catered for. Towards Lochearnhead facilities thin out, though caravans and tents are catered for at Callander and Strathyre. The provision of B+Bs and hotels tends to be more numerous towards Crieff. There is no convenient SYHA.
Geographical Features:- An area of wild country bordering on populated areas with much sheep farming and managed grouse moor, and deer forest. In such an area, with easy access, some control over this access is exercised but this is not too limiting for the visitor. Respect for the land use in the area is essential in order that good relations between landowner and visitor continue to be maintained. This is especially relevant in the sheep farming areas in the following pages.
Mountains:- The area is dominated by Ben Vorlich and its near neighbour Stuc a Chroin, at 985 and 972 metres respectively. The great mass of Ben Chonzie (just a 'Munro' at 931m or about 3050ft.) is the highest of the remaining mountains and more typical of the region, having a mostly

smooth, rounded profile. Indeed the remainder of the mountains lack interest in their upper reaches, the glens are of more interest and variety.

Rivers :- Virtually all the following area is drained by the River Earn. Comrie lies at the confluence of this with the River Lednock from the north and Water of Ruchill from the south west. The Keltie Water drains to Callander and out to sea via the River Teith and River Forth whilst Finglen Burn flows into the Tay. There are no major problems with river crossings in this area.

Forests :- Not much of this area has been planted (yet!) and the main area of forest encountered on the following routes is Glen Boltachan, and here a variety of both natural and planted trees provide interest. The natural woodland in lower Glen Artney makes the exploration of the lower glen track (as distinct from the road) most worthwhile. On the approach to Glen Vorlich (near the Ben Vorlich path junction) the observant will note trees with "foreign" branches, where a seed has germinated in a damp pocket on the host tree and grafted itself on. The result is several alder (I think!) with odd ash branches. Strange!

Lochs :- Loch Earn, best appreciated from Glen Vorlich is in sharp contrast to the other significant sheet of water, Loch Lednock, with its dam, scarring metalled roads, ugly buildings and huge bits of plumbing. The beauty and the beast.

Emergency :- Both Glen Lednock/Ardtalnaig Glen and Glen Artney are long routes through wild country, the former especially needs treating with respect and proper planning - there is little comfort at Dunan! All other routes are within easy reach of occupied houses or public roads.

Callander to Comrie Routes 1

Glen Artney

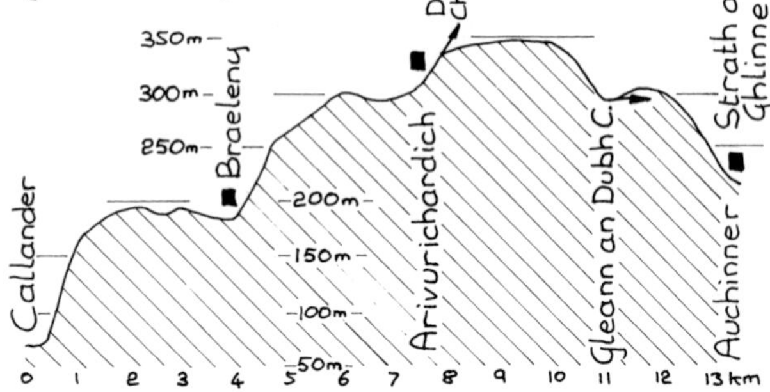

for points X, Y + Z refer Glen Artney 4

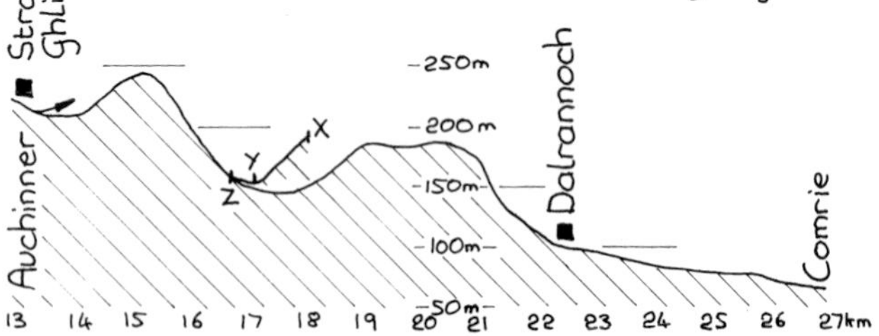

Strath a Ghlinne

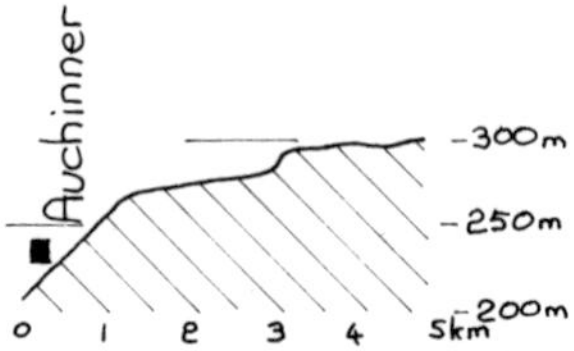

Callander to Comrie Routes 2

Gleann an Dubh Choirein

Glen Vorlich

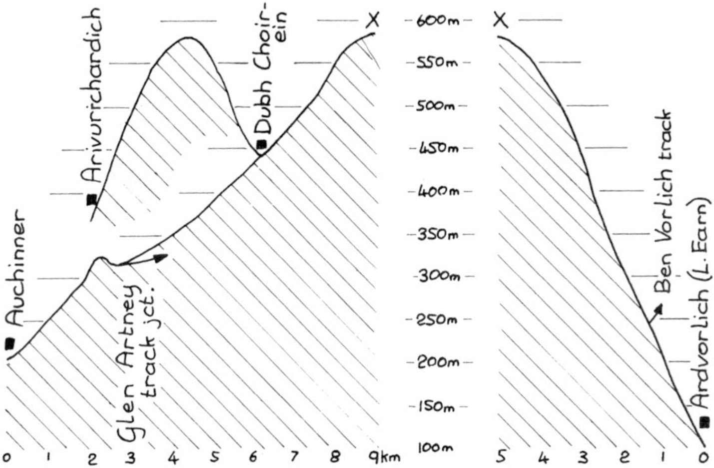

Glen Tarken

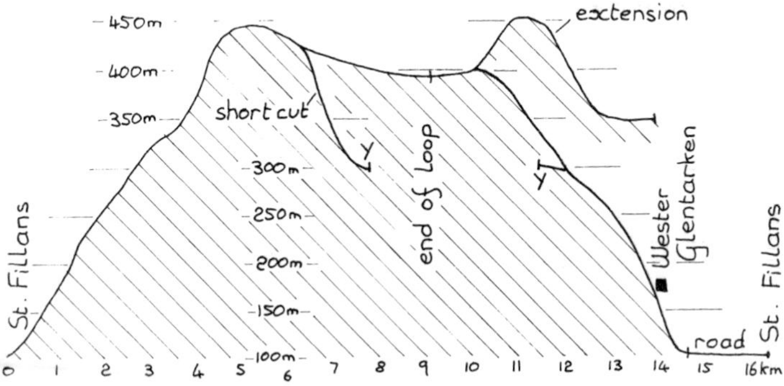

Callander to Comrie Routes 3

Glen Boltachan

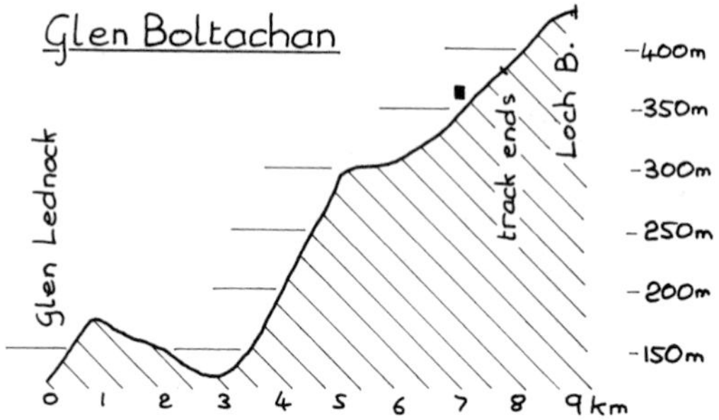

Glen Lednock (loch/Ardeonaig)

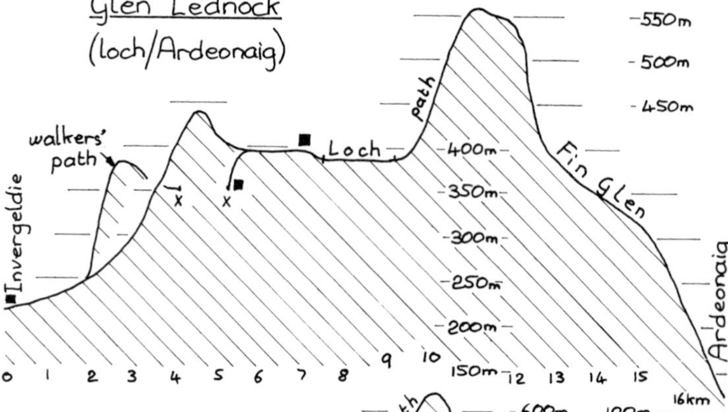

(Invergeldie/Dunan)

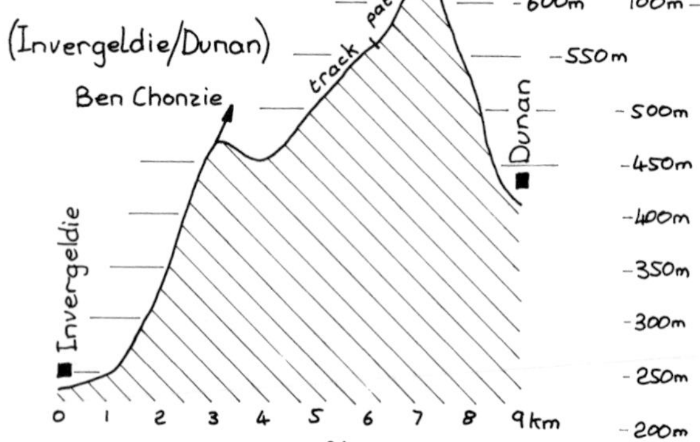

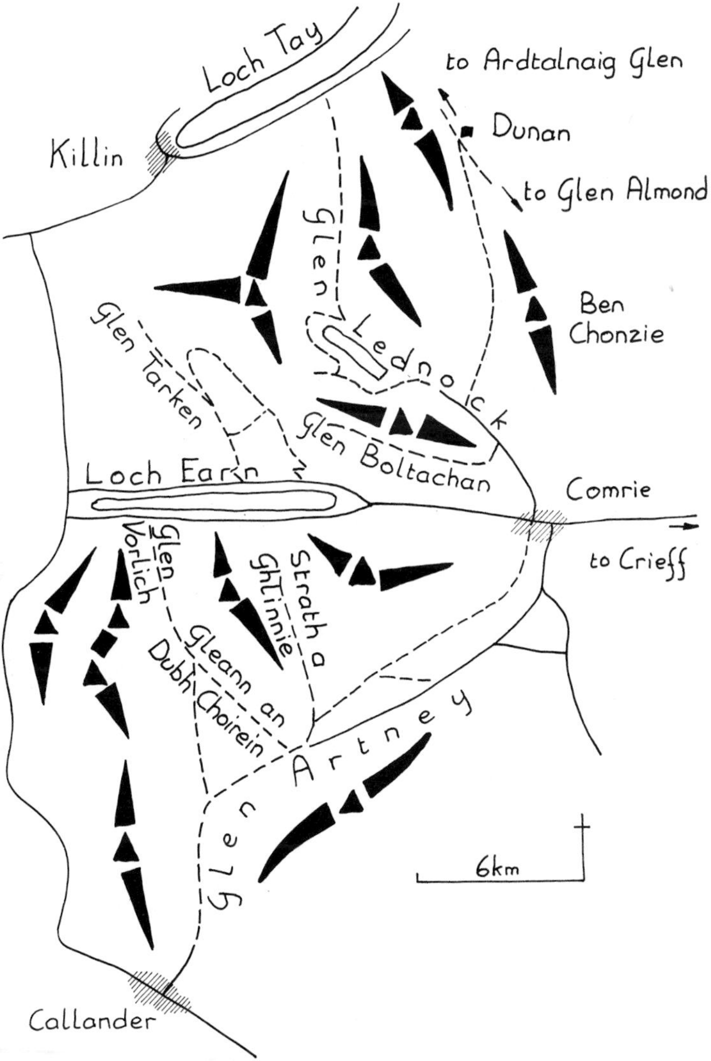
Loch Tay
Killin
to Ardtalnaig Glen
Dunan
to Glen Almond
Glen
Ben Chonzie
Glen Tarken
Lednock
Glen Boltachan
Loch Earn
Comrie
to Crieff
Glen Vorlich
Strath a ghLinnie
Gleann an Dubh Choirein
Glen Artney
6km
Callander

Glen Artney 1

Glen Artney is an excellent through route from Callander to Comrie. Divided into three distinct sections as follows :- the first, from Callander, is not strictly Glen Artney at all, but Keltie Water. However, as over half of this is on a public road all has been included with Glen Artney. The second section runs from the head of Keltie Water to the start of the public road in Glen Artney and includes the start of the side-glens of Gleann an Dubh Choirein and Strath a Ghlinne and the hill path to Glen Vorlich. The third section runs parallel with the public road in Glen Artney giving an off-road alternative to within a couple of miles of Comrie. Virtually all is rideable and this makes a fine walk or cycle ride totalling about 27km or 17 miles - with a cafe at each end - perfect!

Distance table km(m)

Comrie	
	12·5 (8)
Strath a G.	
	2·5 (1·5)
Gleann an D.C. (for G. Vorlich)	
	4 (2·5)
Arivurichardich (for G. Vorlich)	
	3·5 (2·2)
end of public rd.	
	4 (2·5)
Callander	

Public road from/to Callander

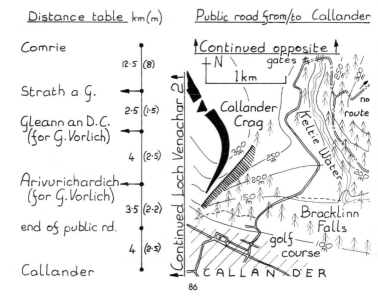

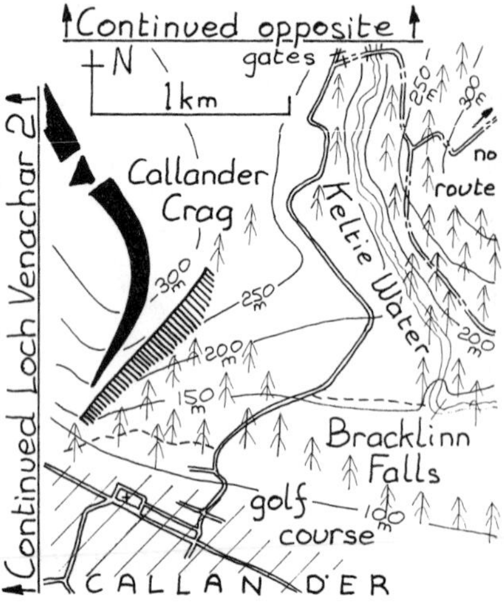

Glen Artney 2

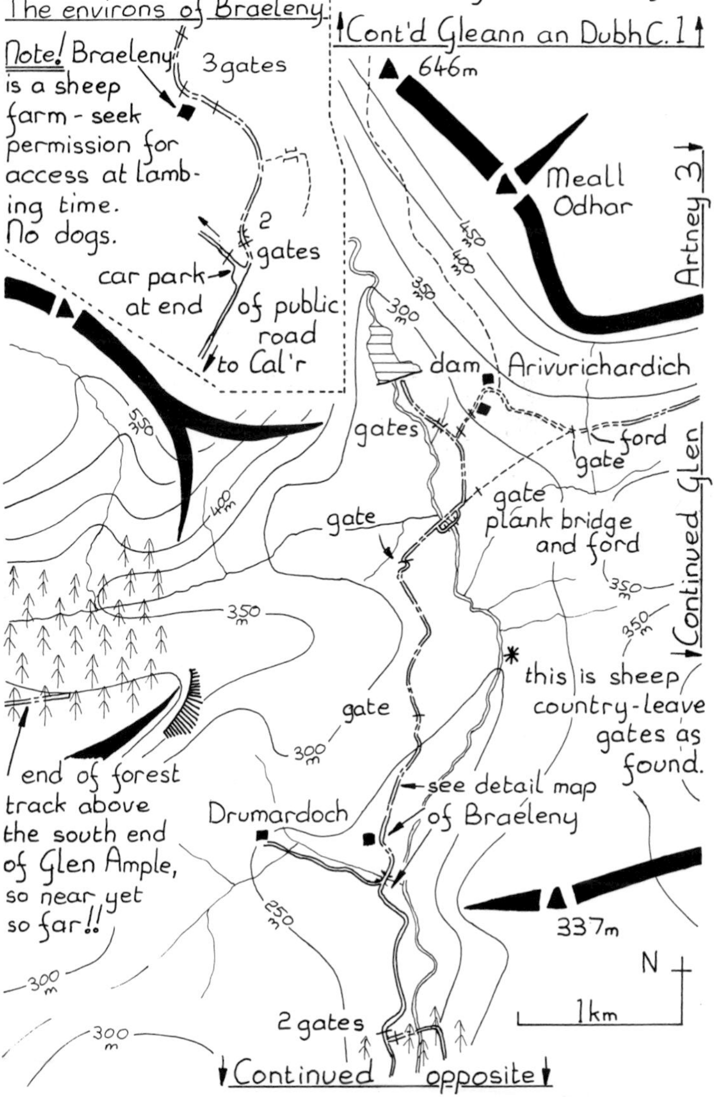

The environs of Braeleny
Note! Braeleny is a sheep farm - seek permission for access at lambing time. No dogs.
3 gates
2 gates
car park at end of public road
to Cal'r
Cont'd Gleann an Dubh C. 1
646m
Meall Odhar
Artney 3
dam
Arivurichardich
gates
ford
gate
gate
plank bridge and ford
gate
Continued Glen
550 m
400 m
450 m
400 m
350 m
300 m
350 m
350 m
350 m
this is sheep country - leave gates as found.
gate
300 m
end of forest track above the south end of Glen Ample, so near yet so far!!
see detail map of Braeleny
Drumardoch
250 m
337m
300 m
300 m
2 gates
N
1km
Continued opposite

Glen Artney 3

Allt an Dubh Choirein bridge

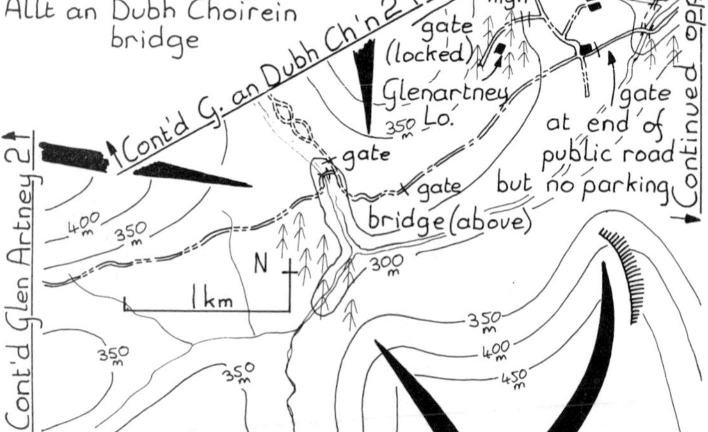

Glen Artney 4

Walkers should use the route from W-Z (or vice versa) using the footbridge to join the public road just above the stone road bridge (just onto the map opposite). Cyclists should use the route X-Y-Z to gain the track down (or leave the track up) Glen Artney.

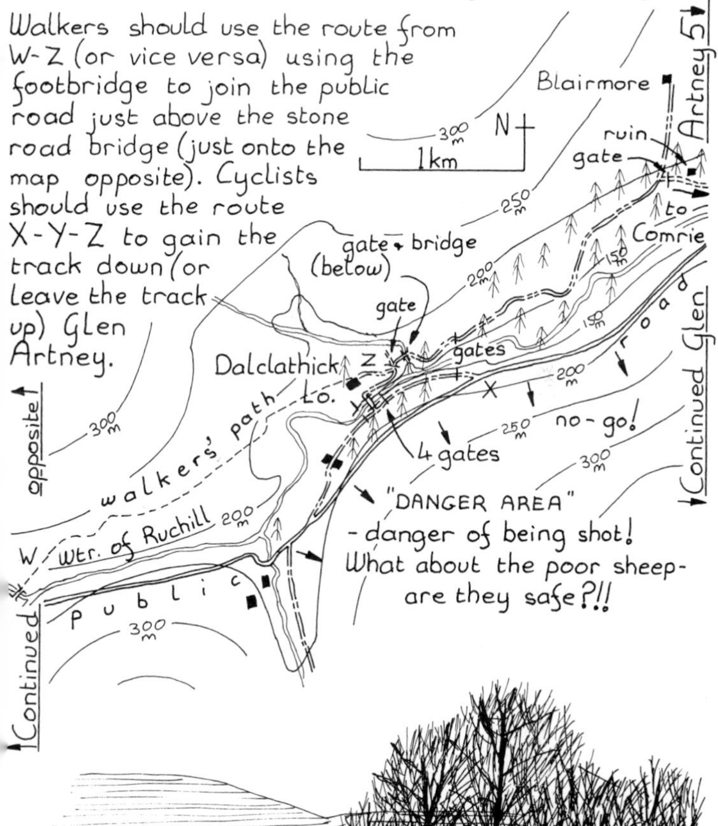

Glen Artney 5

All the roads on this map are public roads except for the track above Dalrannoch. These are included to show the alternative available to cyclists who, if undertaking the return trip from either Comrie or Callander probably would not want to cover the track section of lower Glen Artney in both directions. The public road is almost deserted above Cultybraggan Camp as it serves only a few farms.

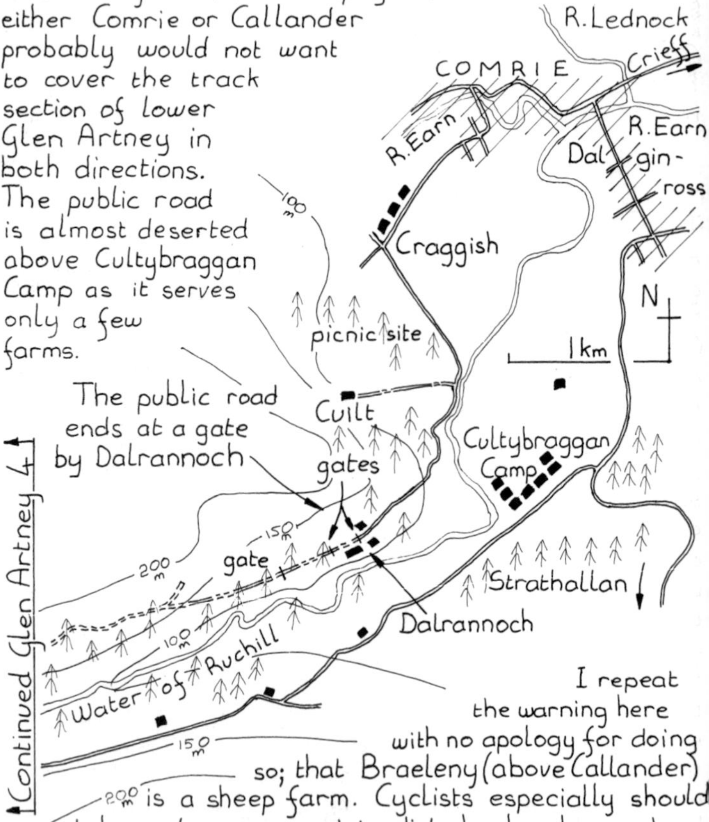

I repeat the warning here with no apology for doing so; that Braeleny (above Callander) is a sheep farm. Cyclists especially should take extra care not to disturb the sheep at lambing time. Either ride very slowly, or dismount and walk, as appropriate. No-one will thank you for frightening the sheep and spoiling this excellent through route for others. Thank you.

Strath a Ghlinne

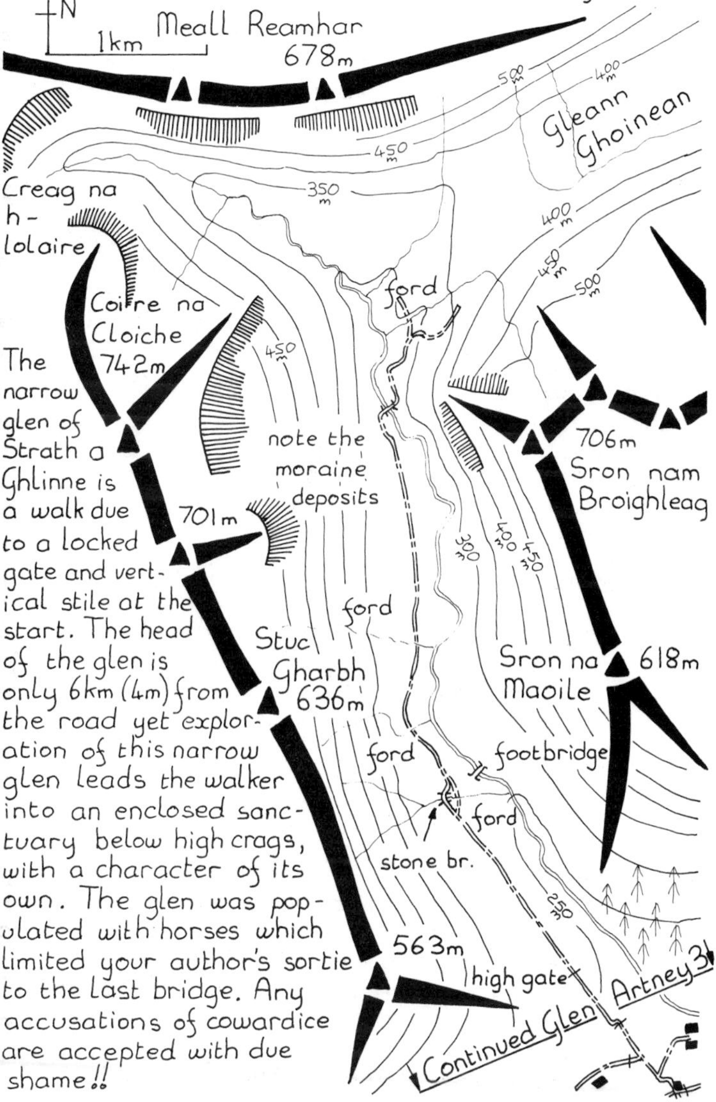

The narrow glen of Strath a Ghlinne is a walk due to a locked gate and vertical stile at the start. The head of the glen is only 6km (4m) from the road yet exploration of this narrow glen leads the walker into an enclosed sanctuary below high crags, with a character of its own. The glen was populated with horses which limited your author's sortie to the last bridge. Any accusations of cowardice are accepted with due shame!!

Gleann an Dubh Choirein 1

The path to Glen Vorlich continues, after the col, about 50-100m east of the burn as it descends. After about a mile it follows the west bank of the burn this joins. The penalty for missing the path is a trudge through deep heather.

↑Continued Glen Vorlich↑

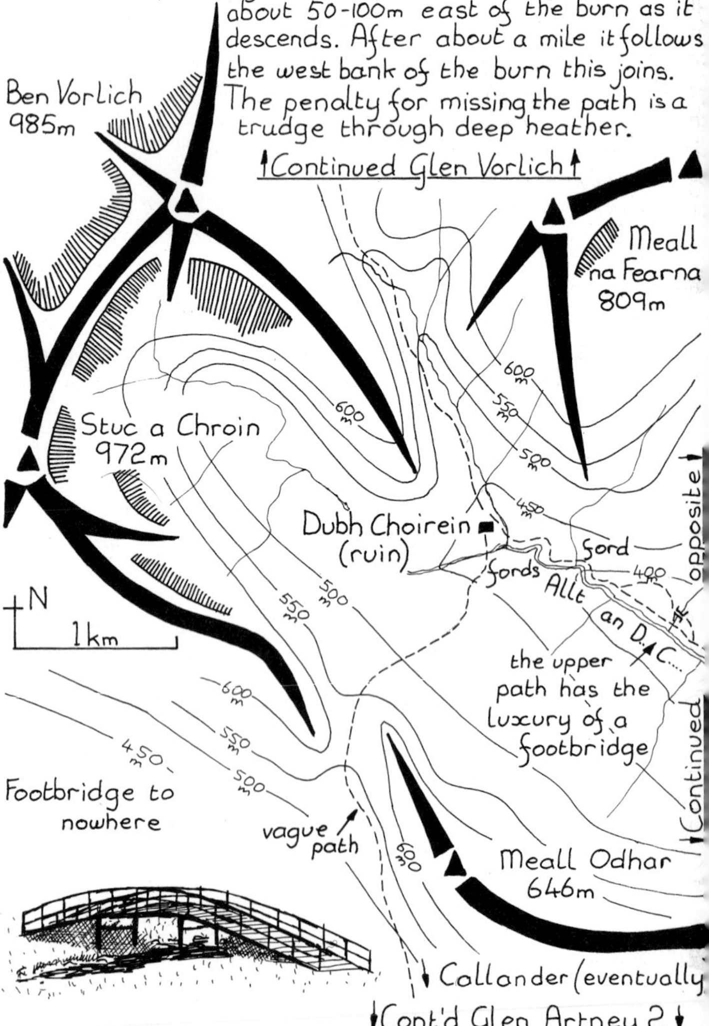

Footbridge to nowhere

↓Cont'd Glen Artney 2↓

Gleann an Dubh Choirein 2

Gleann an Dubh Choirein, although only about 6km or 4 miles in length, is of some strategic importance to the walker. Starting some 2km (just over a mile) from the end of the public road in Glen Artney the glen proceeds north west towards Ben Vorlich. Not only is access possible to the quiet side of this deservedly popular mountain (its finest crags are seen in this ascent) but a through walk to Glen Vorlich may be undertaken though the path over the col is somewhat vague. Also, from the ruins of Dubh Choirein a hill path runs south to Arivurichardich and Callander. A fine horseshoe hill walk would also take in Stuc a Chroin, but this guide is about the glens. A distance chart, opposite, summarises the location of the glen.

The only emergency shelter in the vicinity is at Arivurichardich which marks the Glen Artney/Keltie Water watershed.

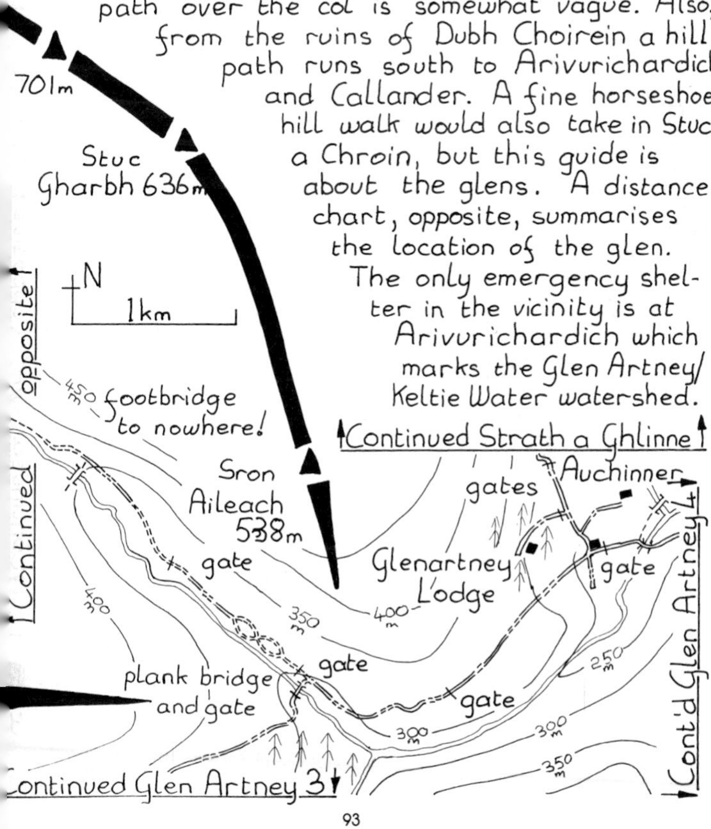

Glen Vorlich

This must be the shortest route to be included! Obviously for walkers only, it is included not for the ascent of Ben Vorlich, for this is a guide to the glens, but for its through route potential in following the path to Callander via Arivurichardich or to Glen Artney via Gleann an Dubh Choirein. The path over the col is vague. At 'X' a sign post points straight at Ben Vorlich " CALLANDER " If the vague path is lost head for the col. See notes on Gleann an Dubh Choirein 1. Excellent sign-posted provision is made around Ardvorlich for the many walkers heading for Ben Vorlich. Start out from the East Gate.

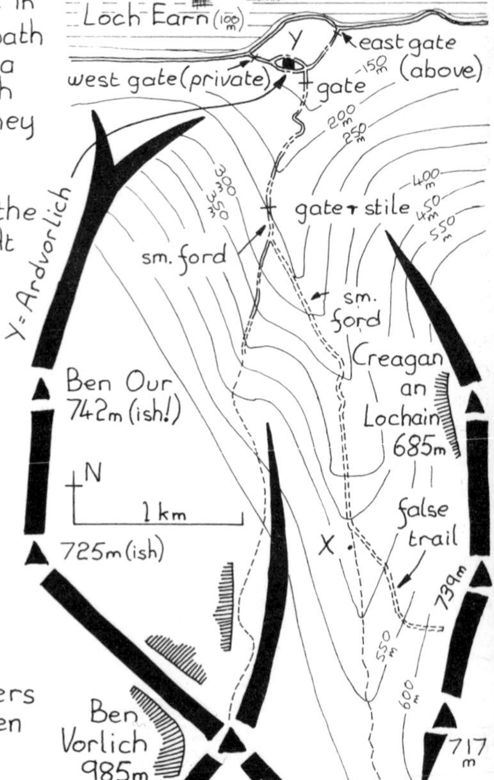

Cont'd Gleann an Dubh Choirein 1

Glen Tarken 1

The tracks of Glen Tarken, above St. Fillans at the east end of Loch Earn provide an excellent day out. After a strenuous climb height is maintained as the track encircles the head of the glen. There is a short-cut between each leg of the loop and a further track extending to a point only a mile from the Lochan Breaclaich track, but it is a rough, boggy mile and a 180m (600ft) climb so the connection is only feasible for those in big boots and a surplus of energy to match!.... and of course, transport from Loch Tay. The more gradual ascent is from St. Fillans and this is also a better track. Care should be exercised on the descent via Glen Tarken as this is a sheep farm - probably better to use the short-cut track to avoid the area at lambing time. The old railway (shown ‡‡‡‡‡) from Lochearnhead is unusable - this would make an excellent cycleway to Comrie. The only blot on the landscape is the caravan site across the loch. Why can't caravans be green/brown like the surroundings they are inevitably put into?.... The loop track from and returning to St. Fillans is 16km (10 miles). The short cut reduces this to 11km (7 miles) and the extension each way is 4km (2·5 miles). There is no shelter in Glen Tarken.

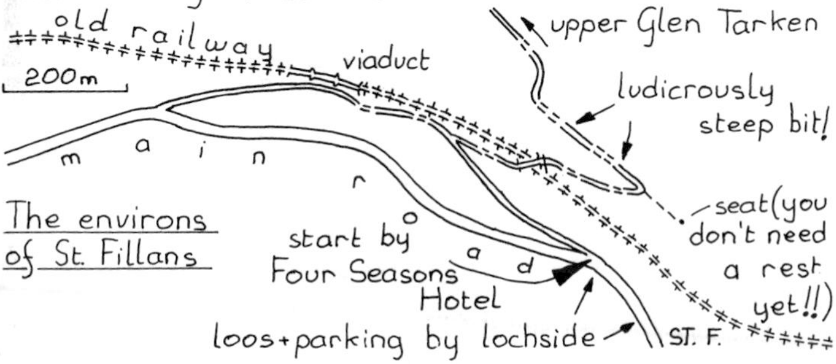

The environs of St. Fillans

Glen Tarken 2

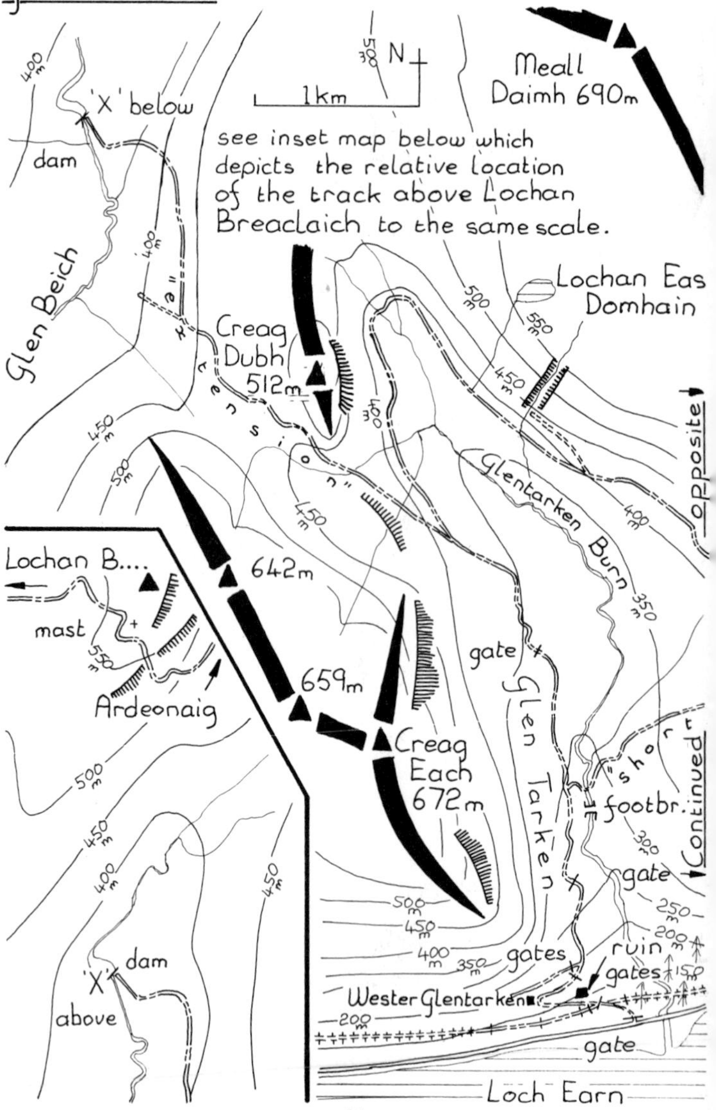

N
1km
'X' below
dam
Glen Beich
see inset map below which depicts the relative location of the track above Lochan Breaclaich to the same scale.
Meall Daimh 690m
Lochan Eas Domhain
Creag Dubh 512m
"extension"
Glentarken Burn
opposite
642m
659m
Lochan B....
mast
Ardeonaig
Creag Each 672m
gate
Glen Tarken
"short"
footbr.
Continued
gate
gates
ruin
gates
Wester Glentarken
gate
Loch Earn
'X' above
dam

Glen Tarken 3

Again the start of the route is on the last page! The purpose of the Glen Tarken tracks was to build and is now to maintain a series of intakes serving Loch Lednock reservoir. (Lochan Breaclaich dam also fulfils this purpose). The proximity of the Glen Lednock and Loch Boltachan tracks is depicted below, alas no easy connection to either exists.

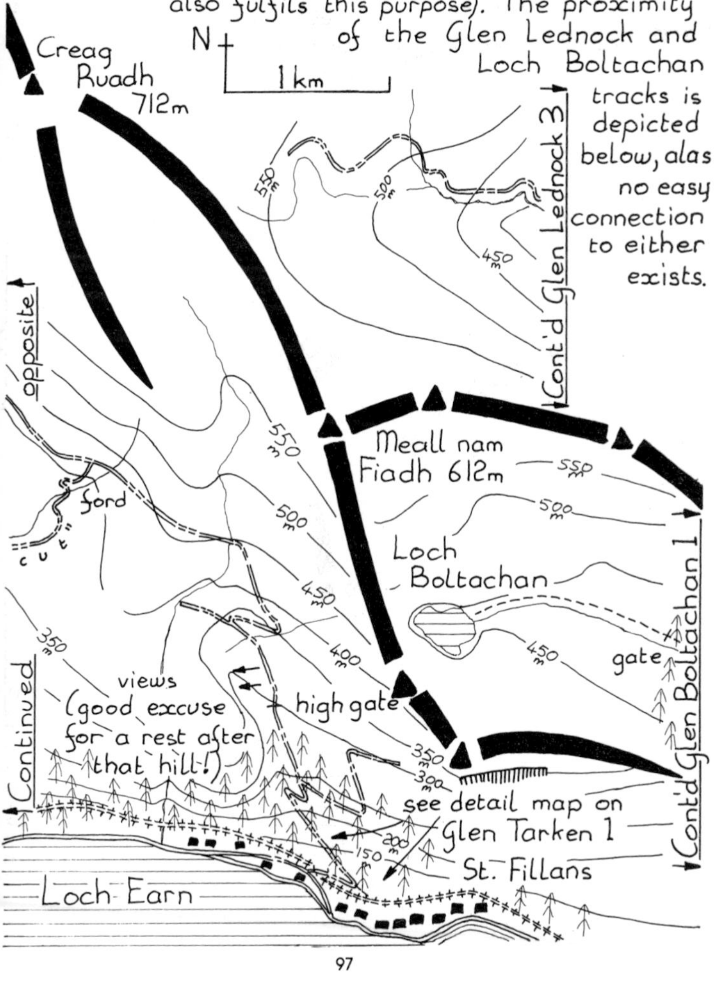

Glen Boltachan 1

The tracks and paths to Loch Boltachan are full of variety. Access is from the Glen Lednock road, the track zig-zags up a grassy slope just north of the monument. It would be presumptuous to assume access is tolerated in the vicinity of Dunira, but stiles are provided along the track depicted here.

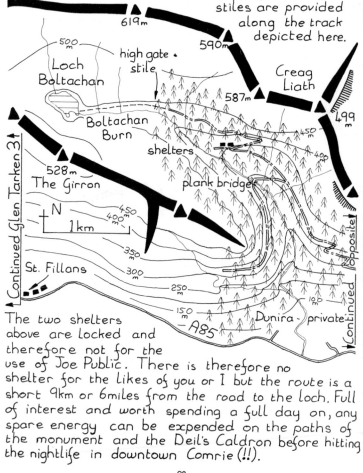

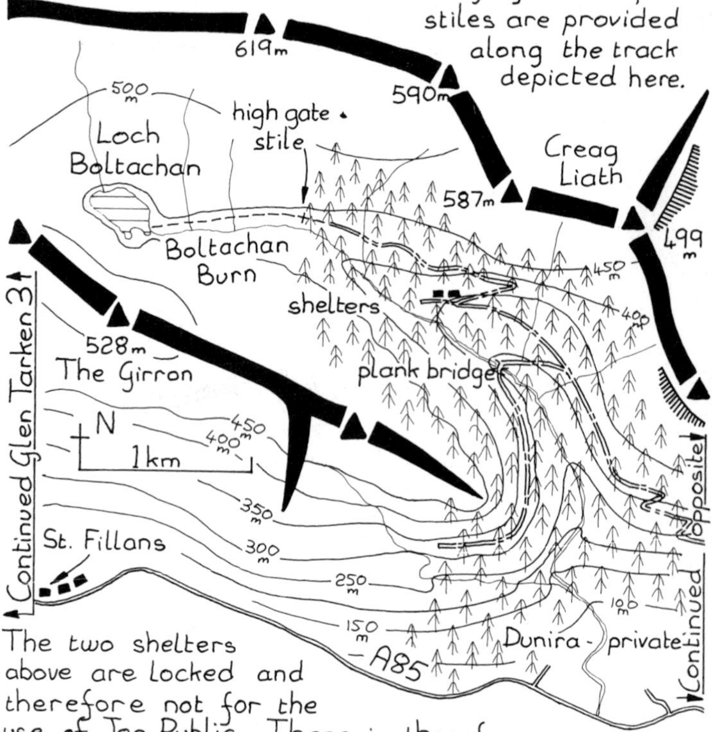

The two shelters above are locked and therefore not for the use of Joe Public. There is therefore no shelter for the likes of you or I but the route is a short 9km or 6miles from the road to the loch. Full of interest and worth spending a full day on, any spare energy can be expended on the paths of the monument and the Deil's Caldron before hitting the nightlife in downtown Comrie (!!).

The woods of Glen Boltachan (opposite) are mixed providing a variety of colour as one looks down from the forest road, approaching the shelters. However the trees do not inhibit the view as the track contours across a steep hillside. From just before the final gate the last km or ½ mile or so to Loch Boltachan is a walk, the remainder being quite passable on a bike.

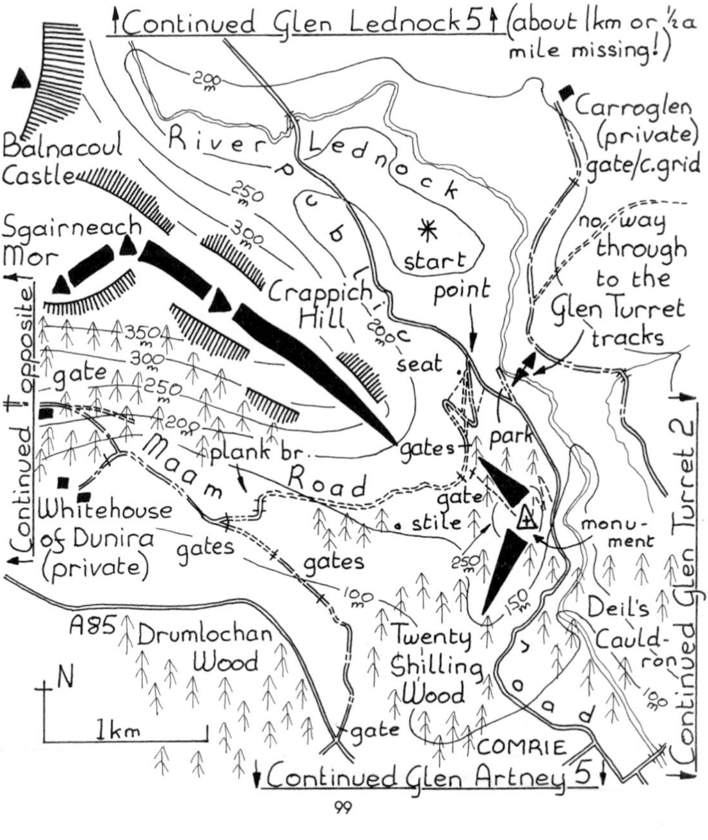

Glen Lednock 1

The Glen Lednock tracks fall into two distinct sections, differing completely in character. Both tracks originate from the head of the public road near Invergeldie. The reservoir roads, mostly surfaced, run up Gleann Mathaig, a side shoot to the south west of the dam. This passes over a low col after a couple of dead-end tracks branch off and heads up to the true head of the glen. From this point an indistinct walkers' path skirts the end of the loch and continues over a high watershed to Ardeonaig on Loch Tay. A bike ride to the head of the loch or a through walk; walkers can cut out part of the surfaced road as shown. The other section of tracks runs over to Dunan, on the Gleann a Chilleine (see Ardtalnaig Glen) / Glen Almond watershed. Basically a walk, though the struggle over the pass with a bike may be justified if part of a longer tour, and there are two options from Dunan as set out opposite. There is no shelter other than at Dunan, which is not, of course in this glen.

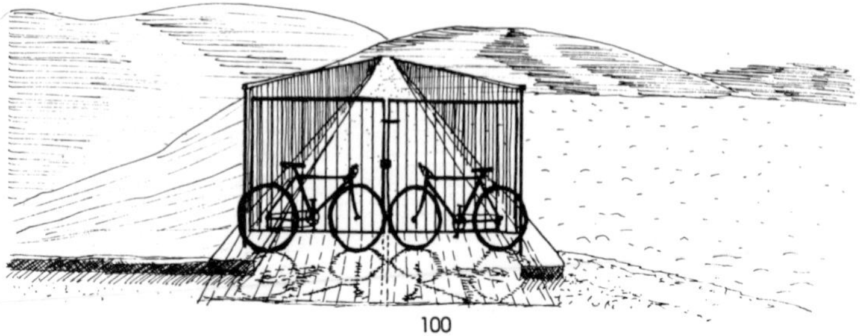

Glen Lednock 2

Whilst your humble author realises that utility buildings have a function to perform there is no excuse for this edifice at the head of Loch Lednock. It must be the Hydro Electric entry for the "Ugliest Building in Scotland" competition! Surely, any building situated in an otherwise wild area should be designed with just a tiny bit of thought for its appearance. The surrounding area is an unkempt mess – the dam looks almost elegant by comparison. Not good enough.

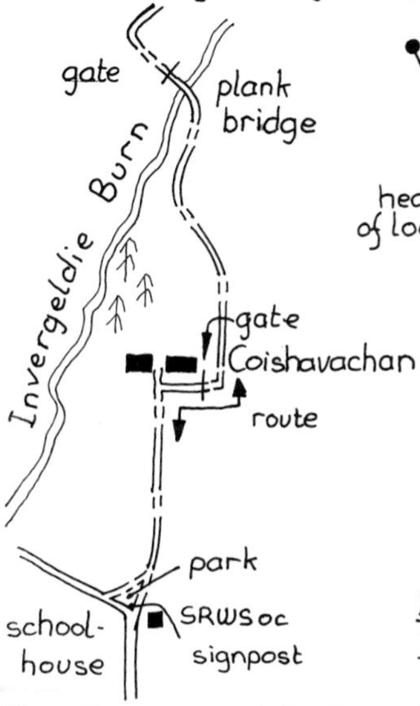

The Environs of Invergeldie

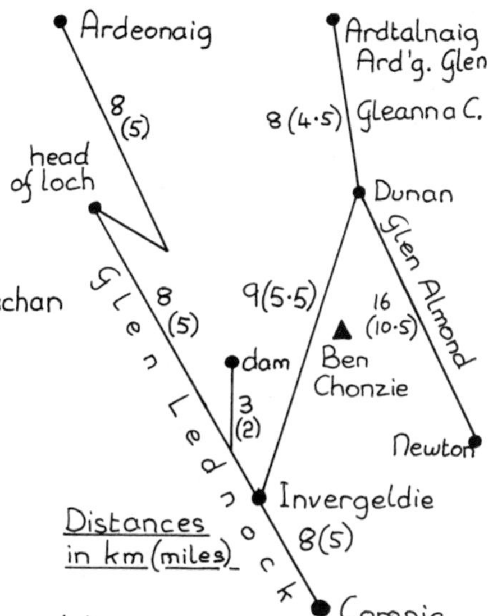

Glen Lednock 3

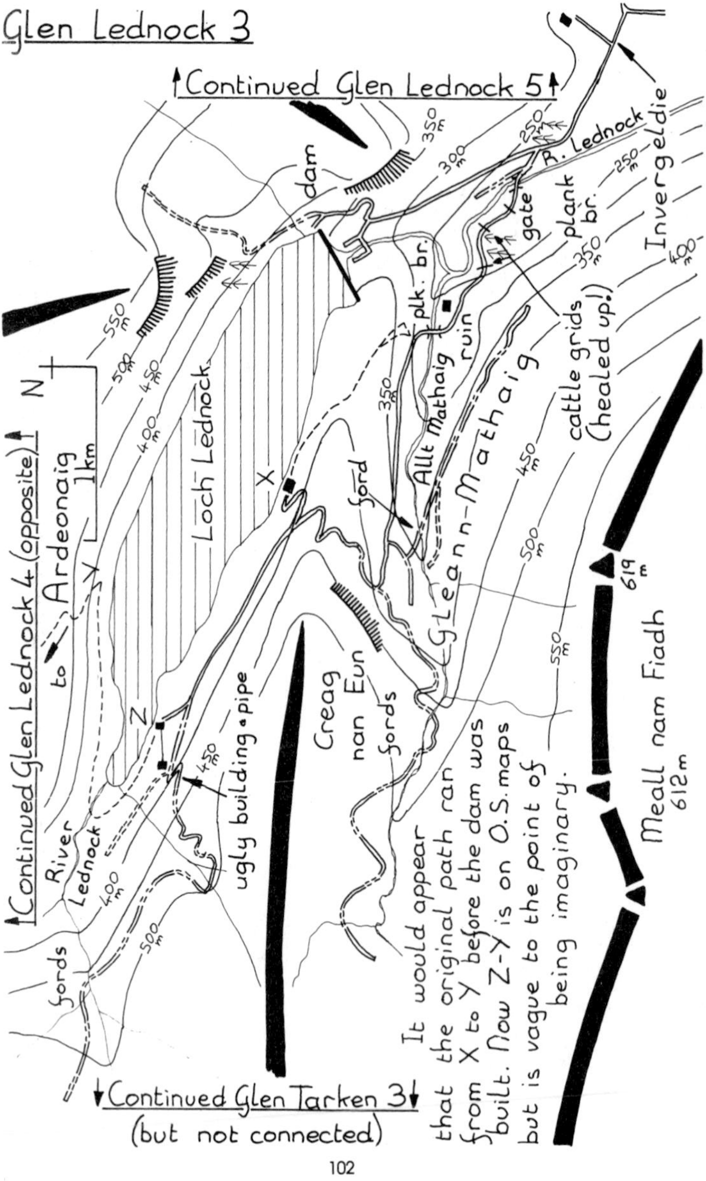
Continued Glen Lednock 5
Continued Glen Lednock 4 (opposite)
Continued Glen Tarken 3
(but not connected)
to Ardeonaig
N
1km
dam
R. Lednock
Invergeldie
gate
plank br.
plk. br.
ruin
cattle grids (healed up!)
Allt Mathaig
Gleann-Mathaig
Loch Lednock
X
Y
Z
ford
fords
Creag nan Eun
ugly building & pipe
River Lednock
619m
Meall nam Fiadh 612m
250m
300m
350m
400m
450m
500m
550m
It would appear that the original path ran from X to Y before the dam was built. Now Z-Y is on O.S. maps but is vague to the point of being imaginary.

Glen Lednock 4

The Fin Glen path needs using, or it will be lost. Despite being rudely interrupted by Loch Lednock Reservoir this path provides yet another route from the south shore of Loch Tay.

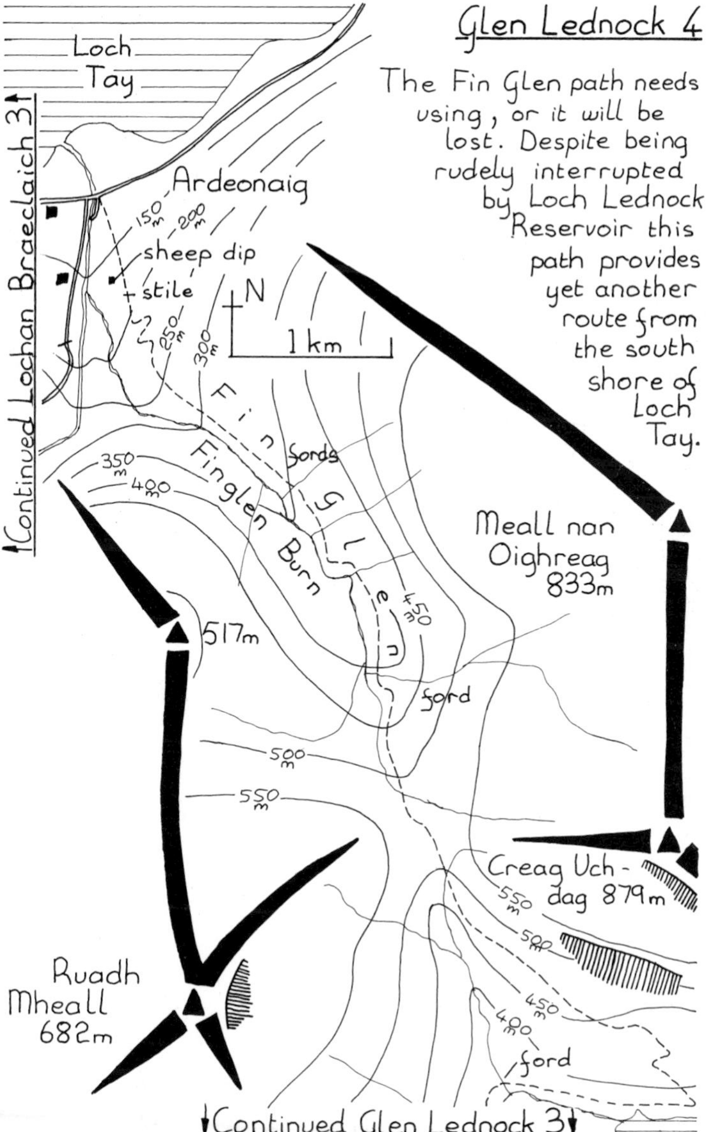

Continued Lochan Breaclaich 3

Continued Glen Lednock 3

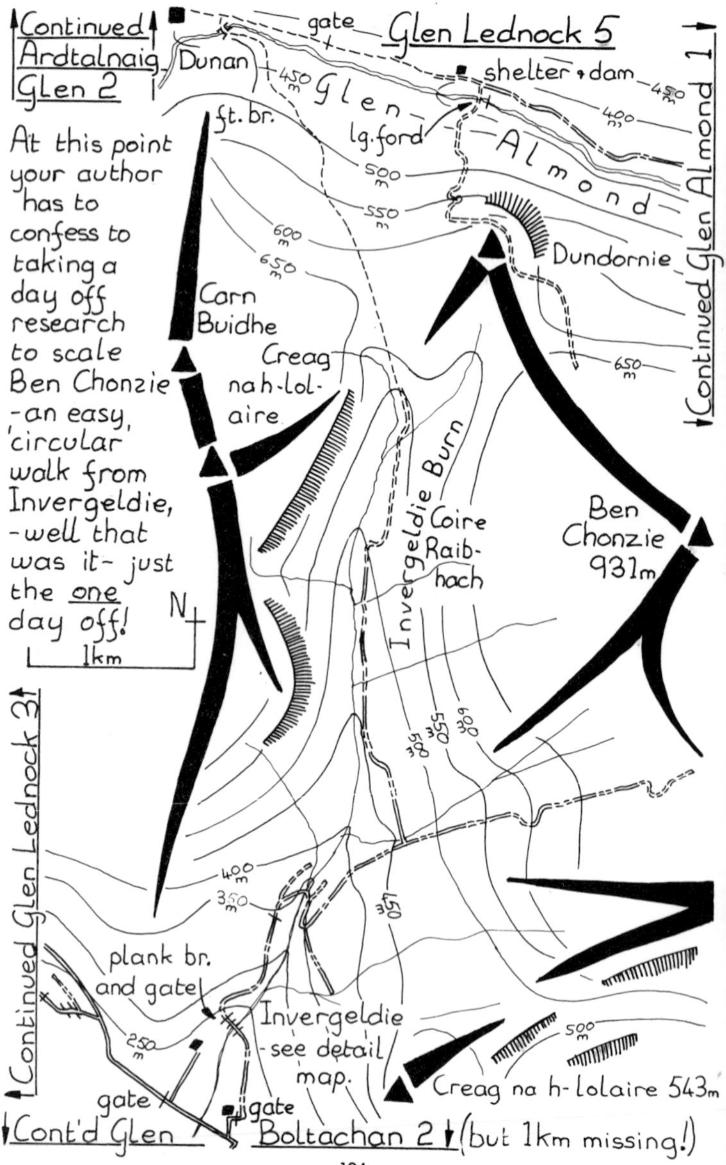
Glen Lednock 5
Continued Ardtalnaig Glen 2
Continued Glen Almond 1
Continued Glen Lednock 3
Cont'd Glen Boltachan 2 (but 1km missing!)
At this point your author has to confess to taking a day off research to scale Ben Chonzie - an easy, 'circular' walk from Invergeldie, - well that was it - just the one day off!
N
1km
gate
Dunan
shelter + dam
ft. br.
lg. ford
Glen Almond
Dundornie
Carn Buidhe
Creag na h-lol-aire
Invergeldie Burn
Coire Raib-hach
Ben Chonzie 931m
plank br. and gate
Invergeldie - see detail map.
gate
gate
Creag na h-Iolaire 543m
450 m
400 m
500 m
550 m
600 m
650 m
350 m
250 m

Crieff
and the
Ochil Hills

Crieff and the Ochil Hills

Access:- This region is the most accessible of all as the A9 passes between the northern extremities and the Ochil Hills. Carron Valley, detached from the remainder of the region (and the rest of this book!) is easily within cycling distance of both Stirling and Glasgow. This ease of access to so many has caused some problems for landowners, thanks to the thoughtless few, resulting in restrictions to cycle access in some areas. That said, the routes that are available give varied standards of cycling, from a long sortie up Glen Almond to a family potter around Carron Valley. Where cycle access is restricted the tracks make fine walks. If, like your author, just being there is more important than the means of travel, these restrictions don't matter too much! Environmentally, the accessibility of these routes from nearby population centres is good, there is no need to drive many miles to get to our "green" activity. It is the car-miles that cause the damage to the fresh air we seek to enjoy. I digress!

Accommodation:- All-year tourist info. centres at Crieff, Stirling and Auchterarder will give details of the ample choice in this area. Caravanning or camping at Crieff may be the best bet whilst the Youth Hostel at Glen Devon makes an ideal base from which to explore the Ochil Hills.

Geographical Features:- The mountains in the north and west of the region give way to much enclosed land to the south and east, this being relieved by the Ochil Hills, Fintry Hills and Kilsyth Hills.

Mountains:- Glen Almond passes north of the only Munro in the region, Ben Chonzie. The remaining heights are mostly heather clad grouse moor rising to around 600m or 2000ft. The Ochil Hills are in vivid contrast with their striking southern escarpment and steep sided, yet rounded hills. This is hillwalkers' country though Glen Devon and Glen Sherup provide reasonable bike tracks, and an introduction to the area.

Rivers:- The rivers Almond and Tay collect the north of the region's precipitation which flows via Perth into the Firth of Tay. The River Devon flows south east, then west to the Forth entering the latter east of Stirling. Also entering the Firth of Forth, at Grangemouth is the River Carron. The Crieff/Auchterarder region, north of the Ochil Hills is drained by the Earn, en route to the Tay, and by Allan Water south to the Forth. None of the routes in this section have other than minor fords to cross, such is the provision of bridges.

Forests:- Apart from some new planting around Glen Turret (1994) the only extensive areas of forest are Carron Valley and the lopsided plantation in Glen Sherup. There are some smaller forests in the Ochils but the tracks are too limited to provide decent routes - and certainly don't require a guide book! Natural woodland, sadly, is conspicuous only by its absence - another consequence of a relatively highly populated region.

Lochs:- All artificial! Carron Valley Reservoir has some ducks and even swans but the Glen Devon Reservoirs are unremarkable. Turret Reservoir, about twice the area of the original loch is an extensive and wild sheet of water and gets your author's vote as the best in the area. Loch Freuchie (in Glen Quaich above Amulree) is the only natural loch in the area of any significance.

Emergency:- Most routes are short and never far from a public road or 'phone. However, Glen Almond is a very long, committing route so care is required in planning your route and your timing to avoid your day out becoming an emergency!

Crieff and the Ochil Hills Routes 1

Glen Turret

(Distillery - dam)

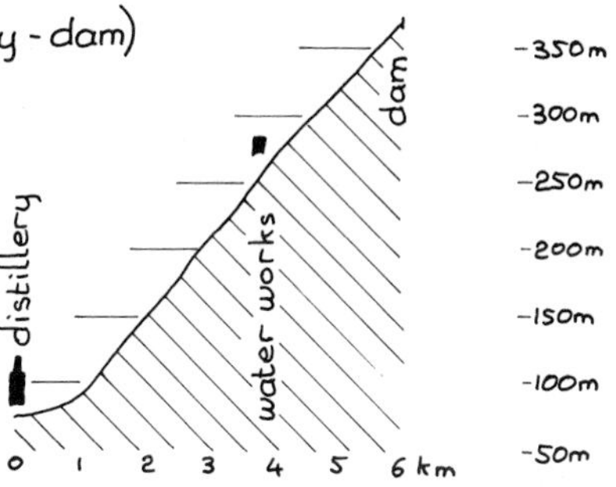

(Dam - Monzie via falls)
(no bikes)

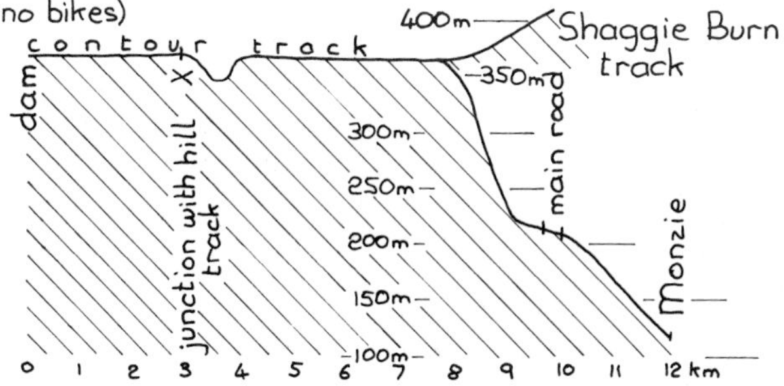

(Dam/reservoir/hill track/dam)
(no bikes)

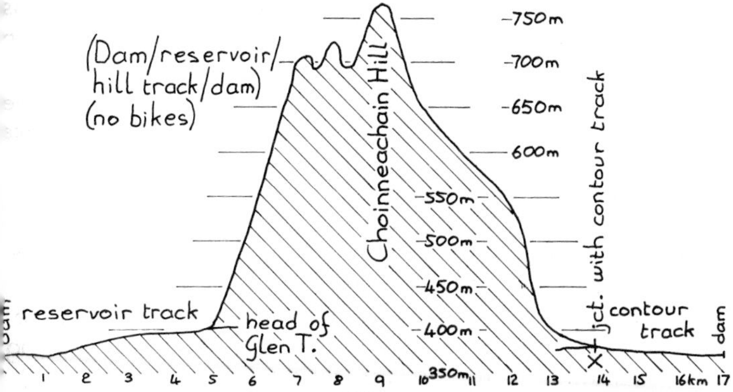

Crieff and the Ochil Hills Routes 2

(Dam-Comrie via Braefordie)

Glen Almond

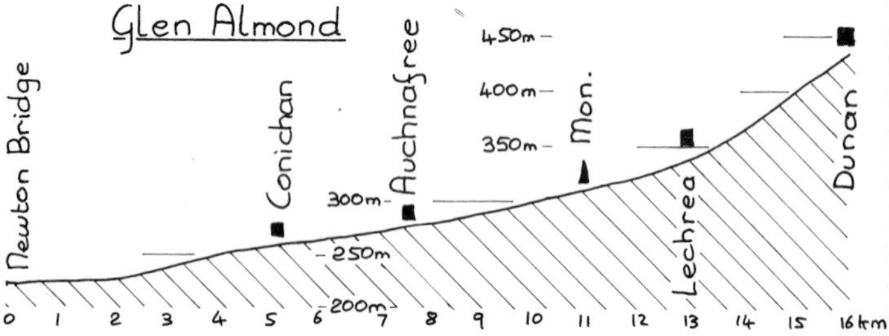

Girron Burn

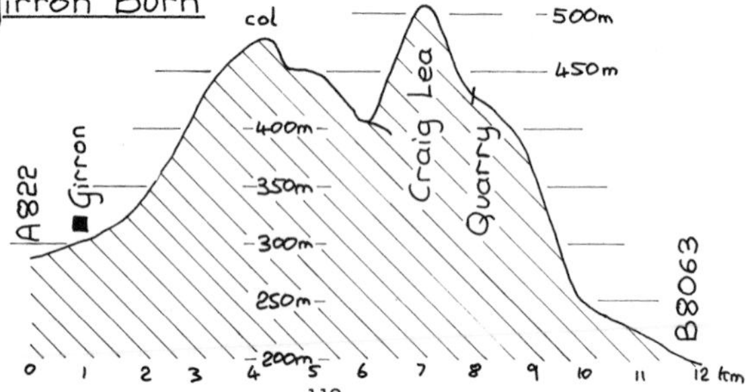

Crieff and the Ochil Hills Routes 3

Milton Burn

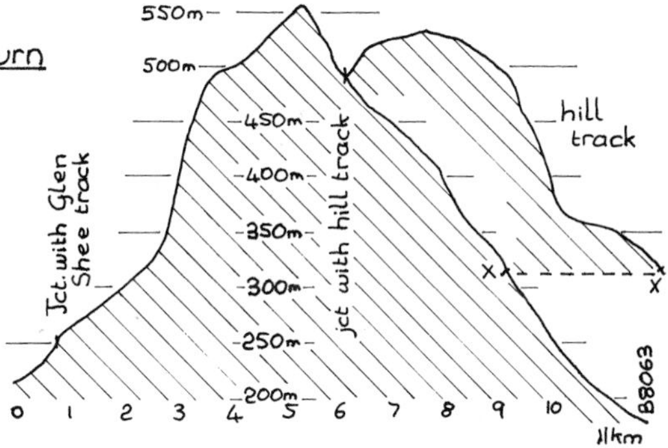

Glen Shee

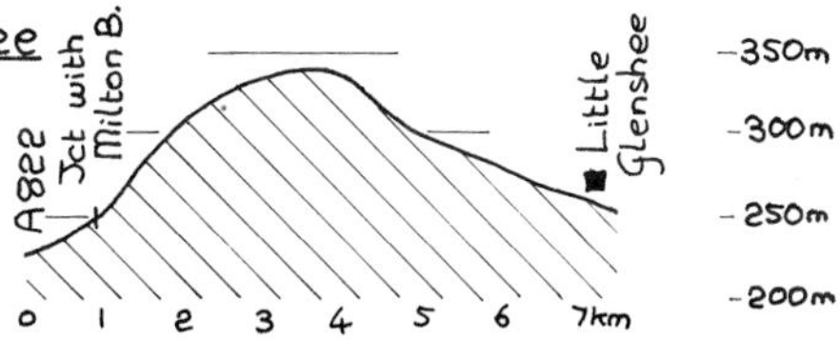

Glen Devon

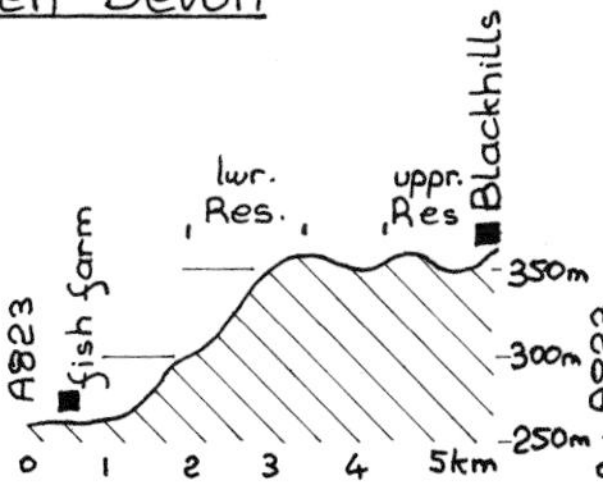

Glen Sherup

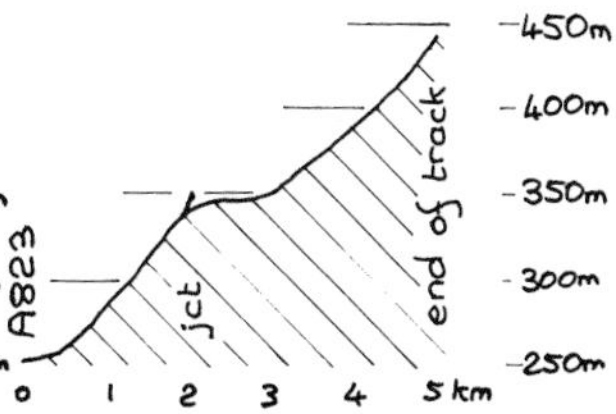

Carron Valley

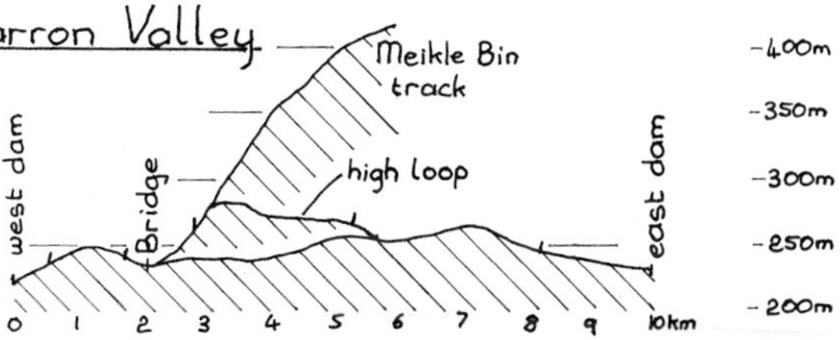

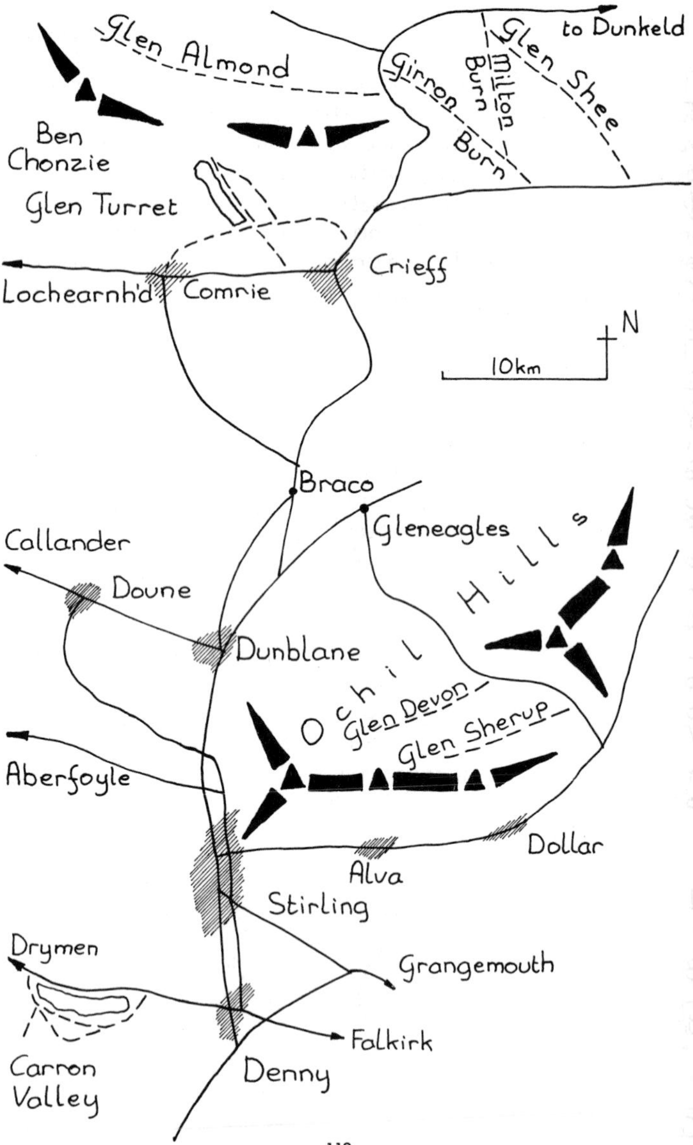

Glen Almond
to Dunkeld
Glen Shee
Milton Burn
Girron Burn
Ben Chonzie
Glen Turret
Lochearnh'd
Comrie
Crieff
N
10km
Braco
Gleneagles
Callander
Doune
Ochil Hills
Dunblane
Glen Devon
Glen Sherup
Aberfoyle
Dollar
Alva
Stirling
Drymen
Grangemouth
Falkirk
Carron Valley
Denny

Glen Turret 1

The Glen Turret tracks are based around the Loch Turret Reservoir road and the associated tracks to the various intakes, plus one high hill track. These are best described in four sections as below:-

1/ The reservoir road, metalled, and despite the intimidating array of "no unauthorized access" etc. signs at the start, your author is assured by the Central Scotland Water Development Board that it is permissible for walkers and cyclists to use the road. There is even a car park at the dam but that's cheating.

2/ West of the above road a track leads to Braefordie and the woods above The Milton with an interesting link to the Carroglen road.

3/ East of the above road contour tracks run via yet more intakes and eventually descend by the Falls of Monzie. Unfortunately cycling is not allowed on these tracks which would otherwise have been ideal easy mountainbiking.

4/ A further track ends above the head of the Loch and returns over Choinneachain Hill, again bikes are not allowed but this track is probably best explored on foot anyway.

Note:— non-intrusive road connections are shown, many of the "tracks" on the O.S. maps are private driveways and should be avoided.

refer Glen T. 4 for distances.

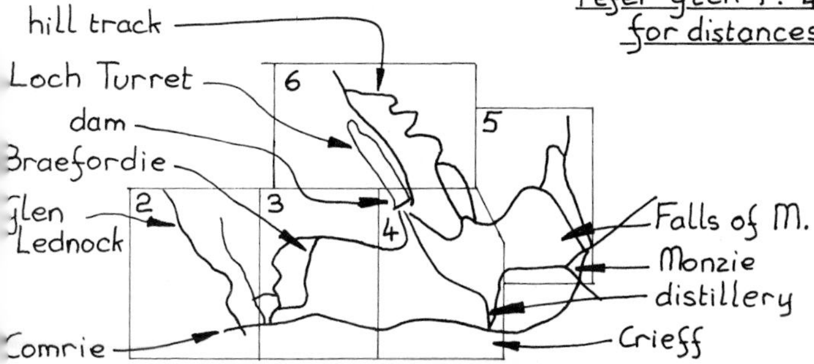

Glen Turret 2

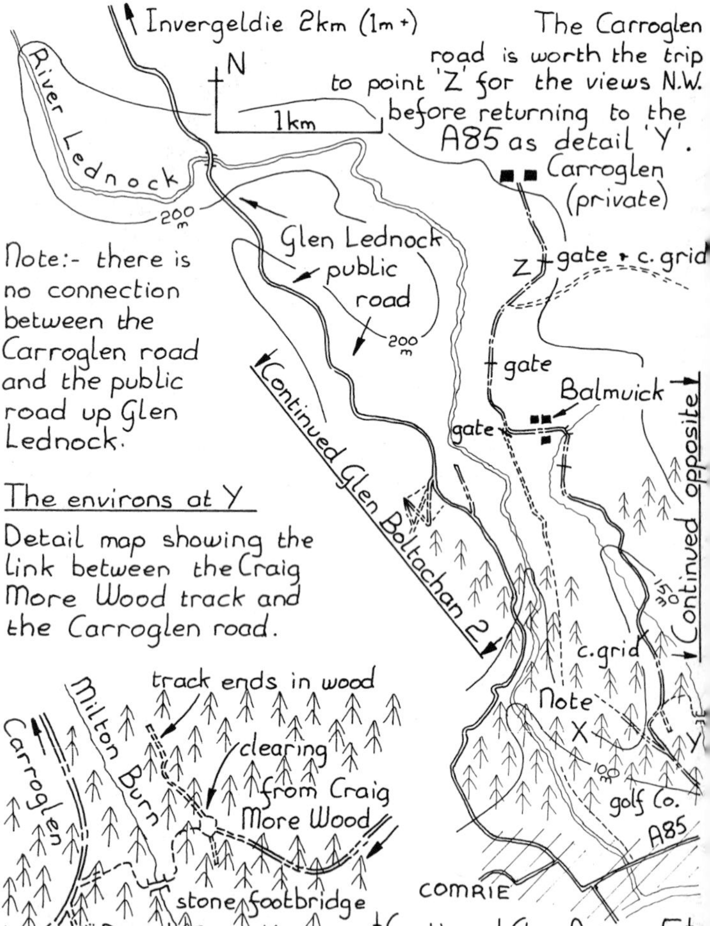

The Carroglen road is worth the trip to point 'Z' for the views N.W. before returning to the A85 as detail 'Y'.

Note:- there is no connection between the Carroglen road and the public road up Glen Lednock.

The environs at Y

Detail map showing the link between the Craig More Wood track and the Carroglen road.

Continued Glen Artney 5

Note X - a network of paths explore the "Deil's Cauldron" and Laggan Wood, all clearly signposted.

Glen Turret 3

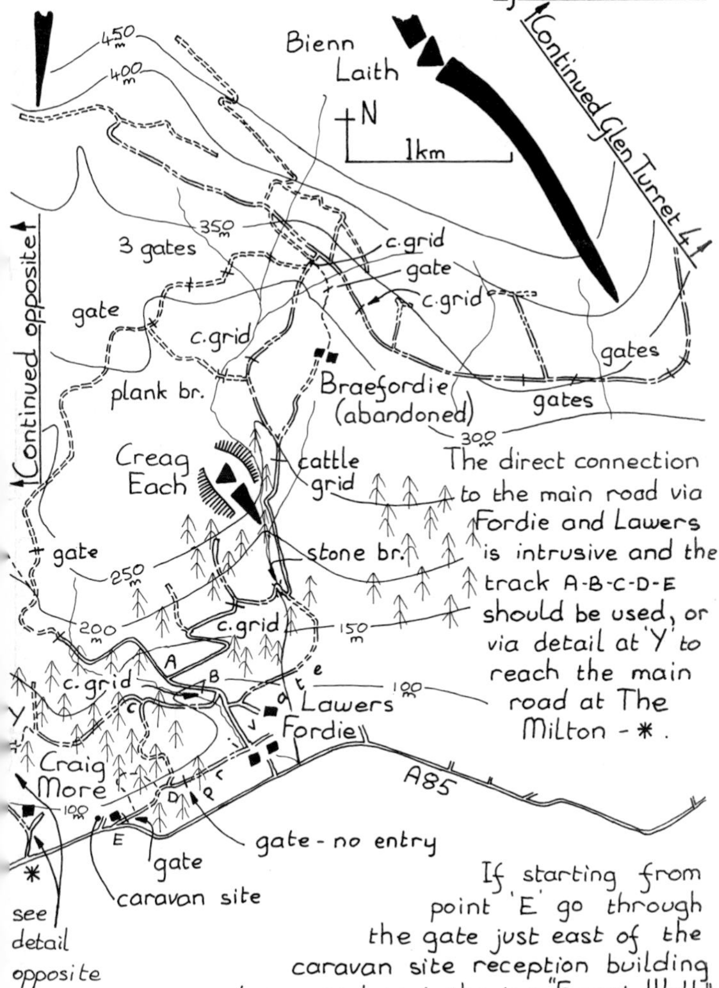

The direct connection to the main road via Fordie and Lawers is intrusive and the track A-B-C-D-E should be used, or via detail at 'Y' to reach the main road at The Milton - ✱.

If starting from point 'E' go through the gate just east of the caravan site reception building and proceed past the two "Forest Walk" signposts on the left. The rough track up to point 'C' is 20m after the second sign. A little care in this complex area is required !!

Glen Turret 4

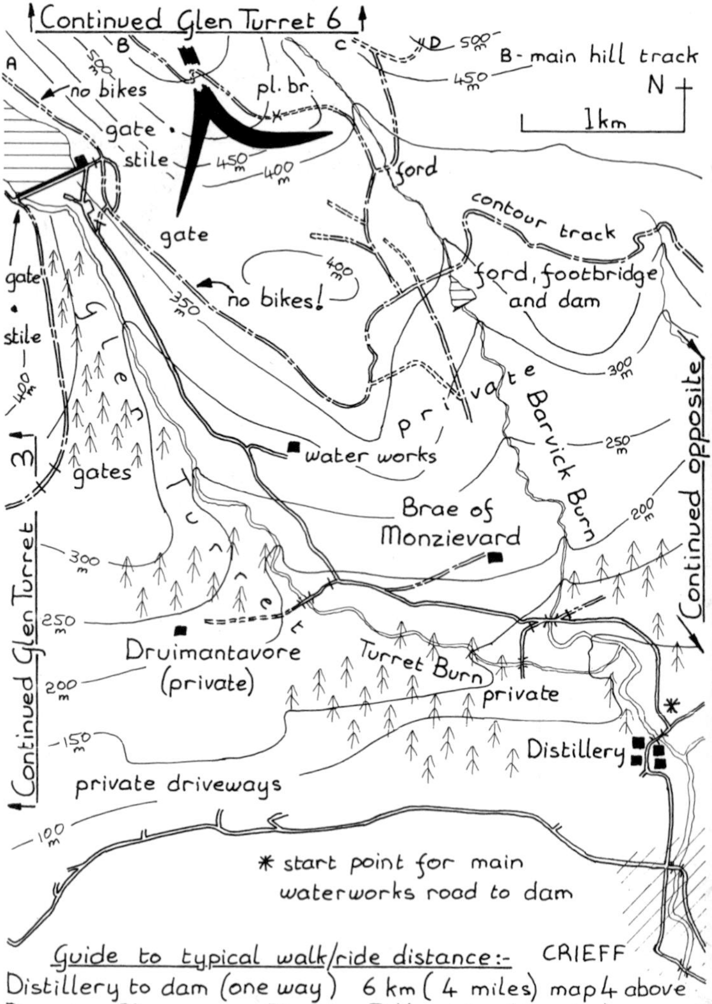

Guide to typical walk/ride distance:-

Distillery to dam (one way) 6 km (4 miles) map 4 above
Dam to Monzie via Monzie Falls 12 km (7·5 miles) maps 4/5
Dam/reservoir/hill track/dam 17 km (11 miles) maps 4/6
Dam to Comrie via Braefordie 12 km (7·5 miles) maps 2/3/4

Glen Turret 5

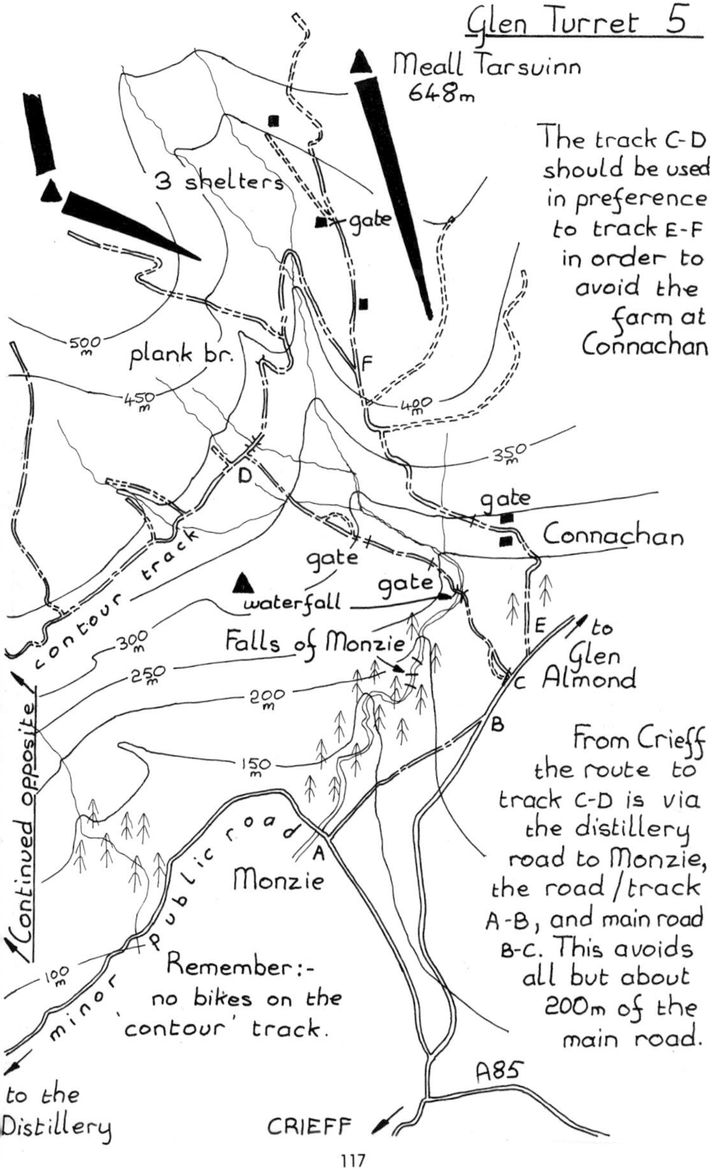

Meall Tarsuinn
648m
The track C-D should be used in preference to track E-F in order to avoid the farm at Connachan
3 shelters
gate
500m
plank br.
450m
F
400m
350m
D
gate
Connachan
contour track
gate
gate
waterfall
E
to Glen Almond
Falls of Monzie
300m
250m
C
200m
B
Continued opposite
From Crieff the route to track C-D is via the distillery road to Monzie, the road/track A-B, and main road B-C. This avoids all but about 200m of the main road.
150m
public road
A
Monzie
100m
Remember:- no bikes on the 'contour' track.
minor
A85
to the Distillery
CRIEFF

Glen Turret 6

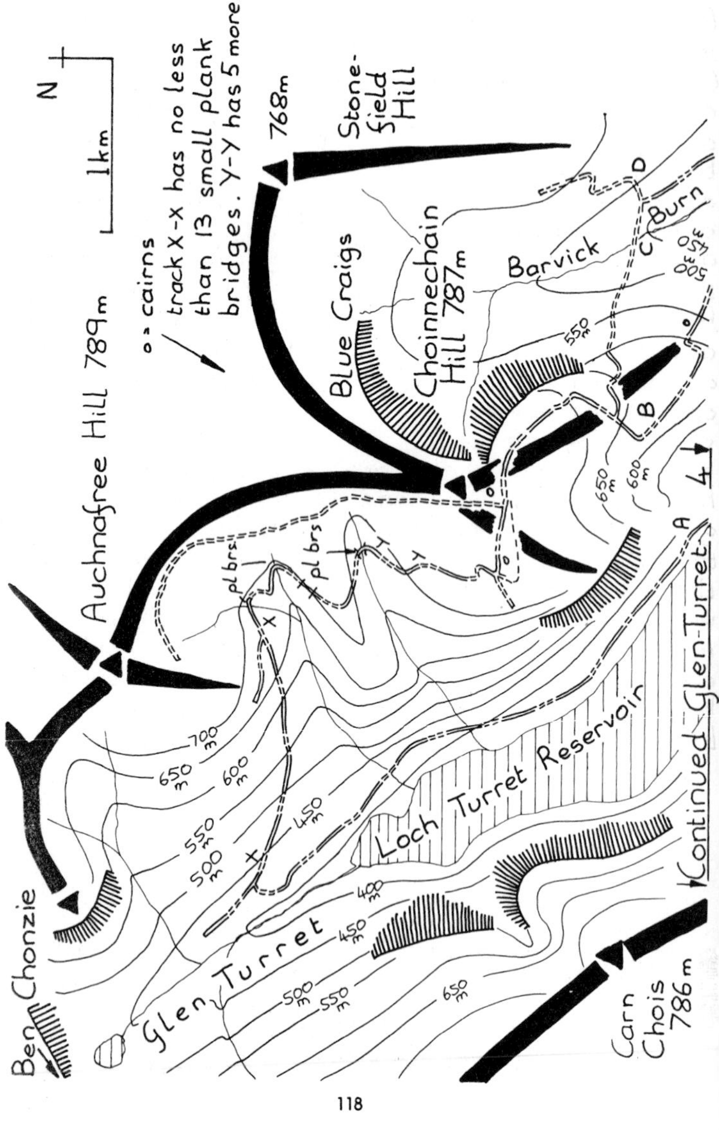

N
1km
o cairns
track X-X has no less than 13 small plank bridges. Y-Y has 5 more.
Auchnafree Hill 789m
768m
Stone-field Hill
Blue Craigs
Choinnechain Hill 787m
Barvick Burn
A
B
C
D
4
pl brs
pl brs
700 m
650 m
600 m
550 m
500 m
450 m
400 m
Loch Turret Reservoir
Continued Glen Turret
Glen Turret
Ben Chonzie
Carn Chois 786m

Glen Turret 7

Although your author is normally opposed to (and therefore does not often include) tracks on the high tops such as those opposite, these are inextricably associated with the Loch Turret Reservoir tracks and, being partly overgrown do not appear the eyesore so many of the newer tracks are. It is also appreciated that the estates have to earn a living and for this access to the grouse butts is required (poor grouse!). It is a pity that the estates cannot derive some income from the use of mountainbikes instead of restricting their use, at least on the glen and 'contour' tracks. The intrusive nature of introducing anything mechanical, even a bike, to the high tracks is fully understood by yours truly. Yes, one occasionally sees a Landrover, but that's different, it's *their land!*

Glen Almond 1

The section of Glen Almond we are concerned with extends from Newton Bridge at the head of Sma' Glen, which is in effect the continuation of Glen Almond, to Dunan, from which links exist to Ardtalnaig and Glen Lednock. The track to Dunan is excellent apart from the last mile. The path to Glen Lednock is for walkers only especially in a southerly direction. From Dunan the Gleann a Chillene track continues to Ardtalnaig. Newton Bridge to Ardtalnaig is 24km or 15miles.

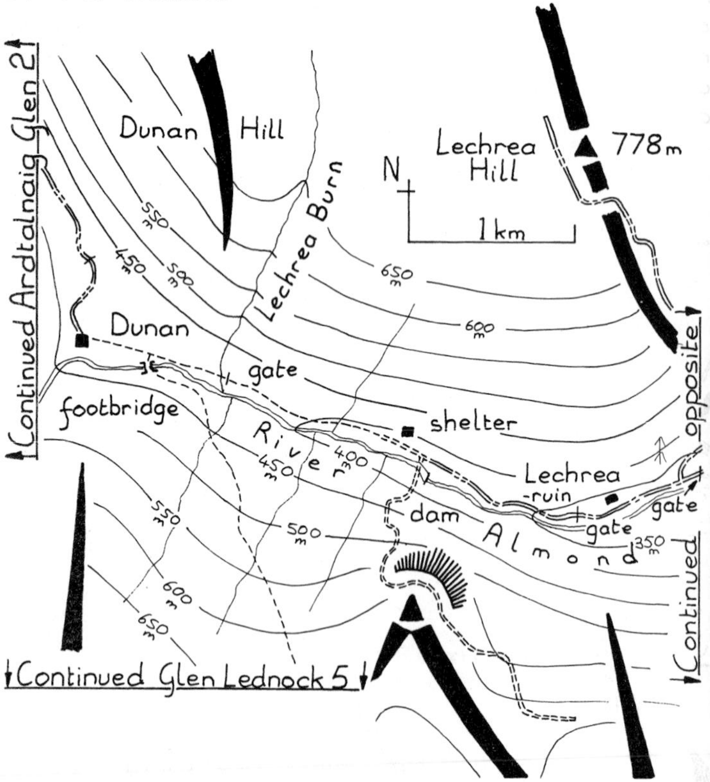

Glen Almond 2

As the Glen Almond track is a right of way and access to the side-glens of Glen Shervie and Glen Lochan intrudes upon the privacy of Auchnafree and Croftmill (in Glen Quaich), these have been omitted. In any event, Glen Almond is the far superior route so my advice is to stay on the right of way and enjoy what is the finest through route in the area. An excellent, strenuous bike ride starts at Newton Bridge, proceeds via Glen Almond and Ardtalnaig Glen to Kenmore on Loch Tay and continues on public roads to Amulree and thence returning to Newton Bridge, a total of some 60km or about 37 miles and including an enormous climb of 420m (1400ft) from Kenmore.

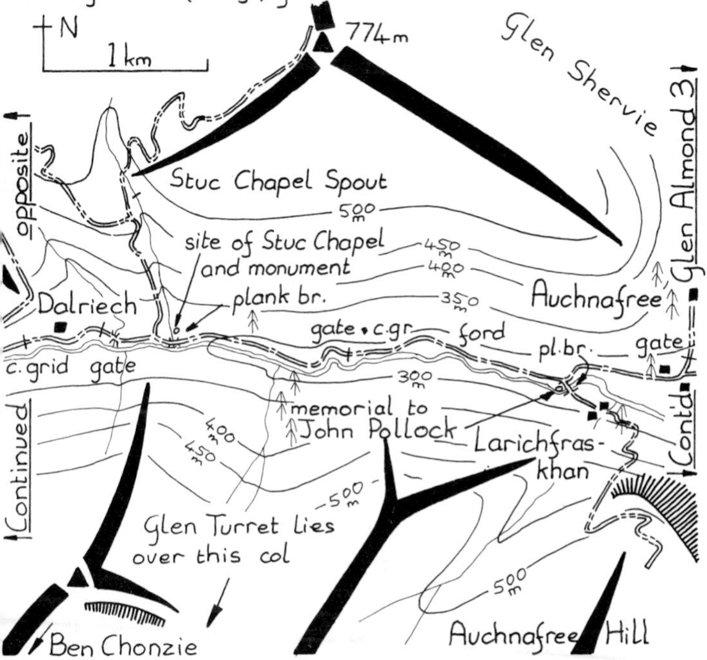

Continued opposite
Contd.

Glen Almond 3

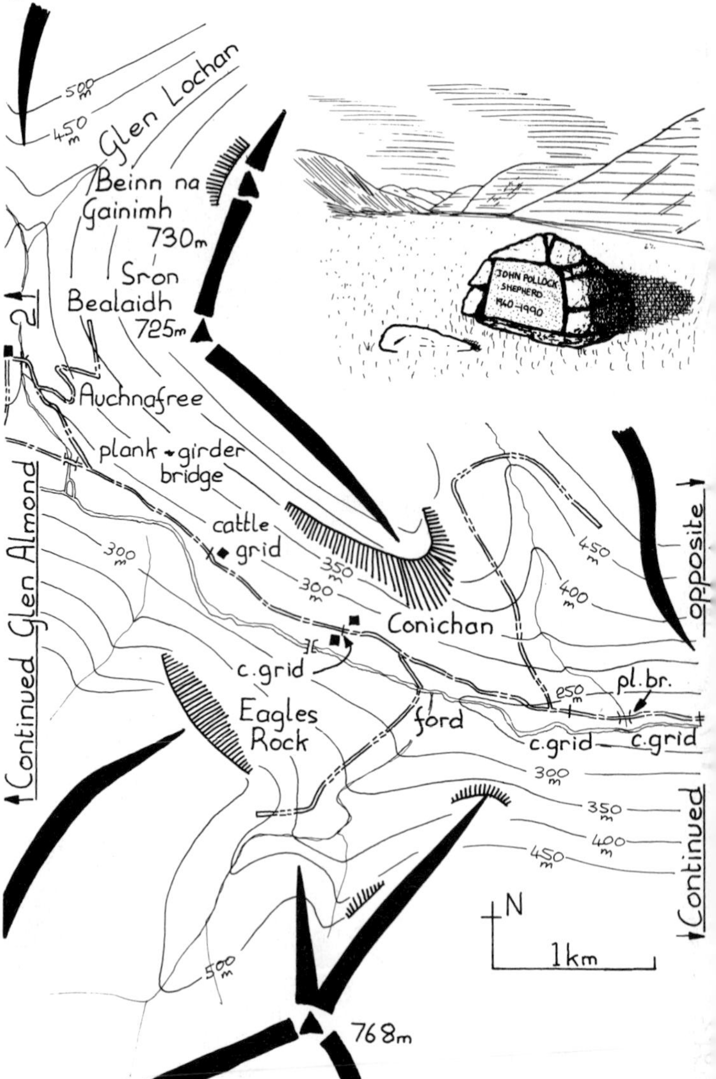

Glen Lochan
500 m
450 m
Beinn na Gainimh 730m
Sron Bealaidh 725m
21
Auchnafree
plank + girder bridge
cattle grid
300 m
350 m
300 m
Conichan
c.grid
Eagles Rock
ford
450 m
400 m
250 m
pl.br.
c.grid
c.grid
300 m
350 m
400 m
450 m
500 m
768m
N
1km
Continued Glen Almond
opposite
Continued
JOHN POLLOCK
SHEPHERD
1940-1990

Glen Almond 4

towards Dunan

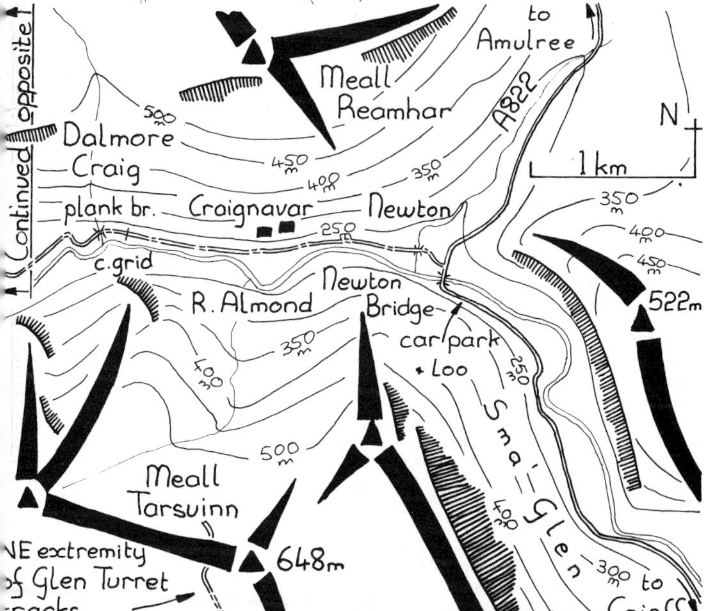

Girron Burn 1

Permission for access to Girron Burn should be obtained from the Keeper at Logiealmond Lodge - the same applies to Milton Burn. Bikes are not allowed and access may be refused during the grouse shooting and deer stalking seasons. That said, these routes are well worth the 'phone call as they both provide a fine walk through wild country. Estates appreciate being contacted and try to accommodate visitors if at all possible. It is indeed a pity that the actions of a few have closed these routes to mountainbikes.

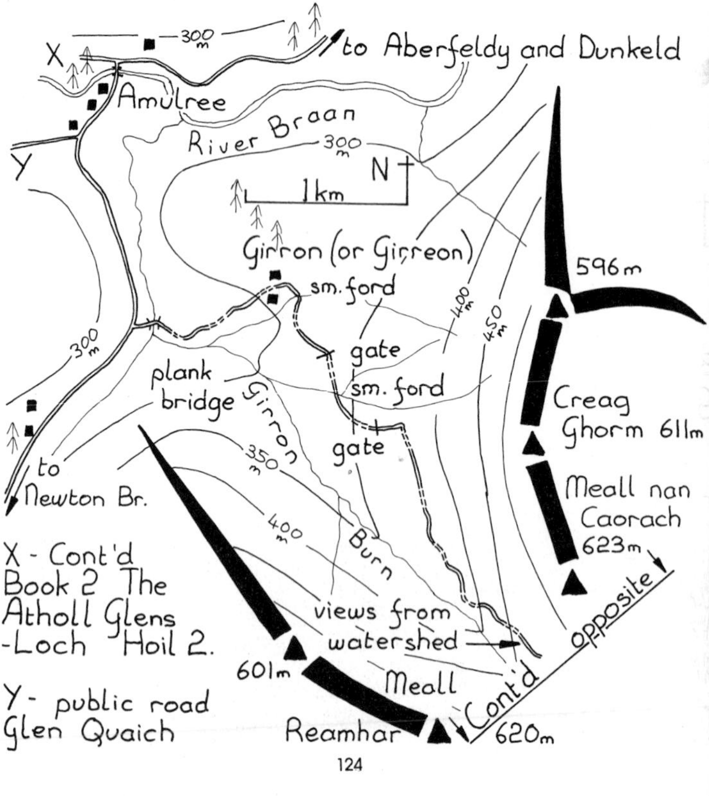

Girron Burn 2

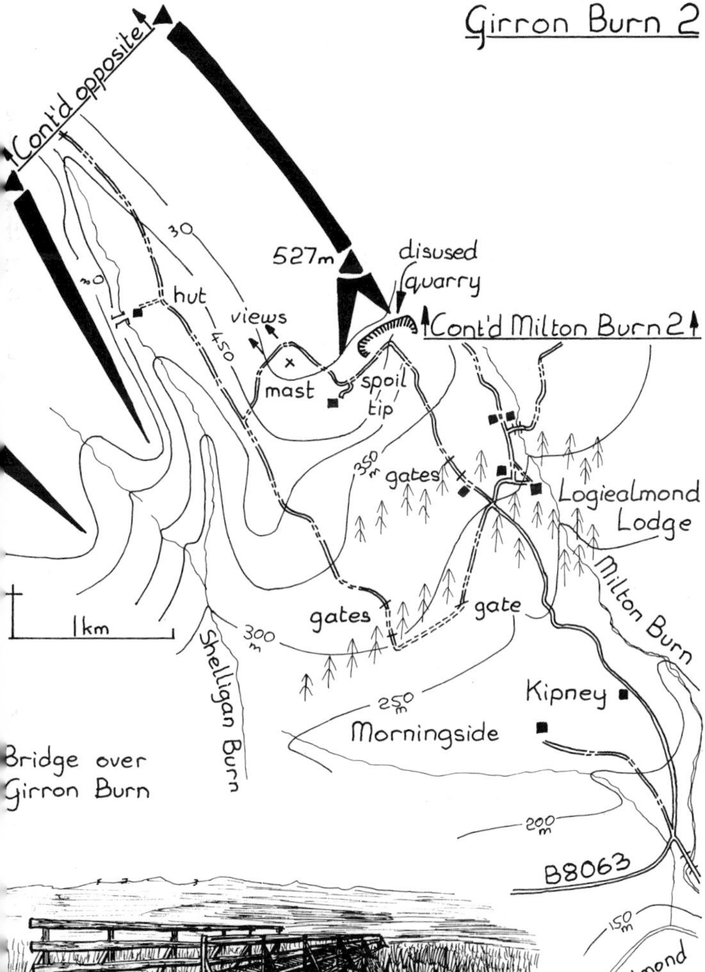

Bridge over
Girron Burn

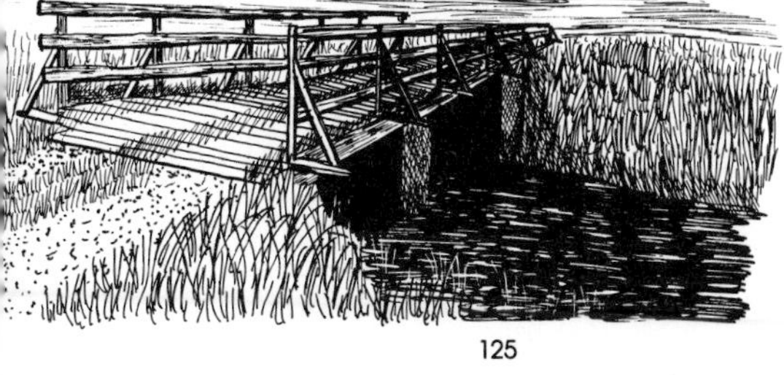

Milton Burn 1

Permission for access to Milton Burn should be obtained from the Keeper at Logiealmond Lodge - the same applies to Girron Burn. Bikes are not allowed and access may be refused during the grouse shooting and deer stalking seasons. That said, these routes are well worth the 'phone call as they both provide a fine walk through wild country. Estates appreciate being contacted and try to accommodate visitors if at all possible. It is indeed a pity that the actions of a few have closed these routes to mountainbikes. The foregoing is repeated without apology :- it is important - no - vital that good conduct and a healthy respect for the estates' working activities is maintained. Even where a route is on a right of way, such as Glen Shee, over, the same respect applies.

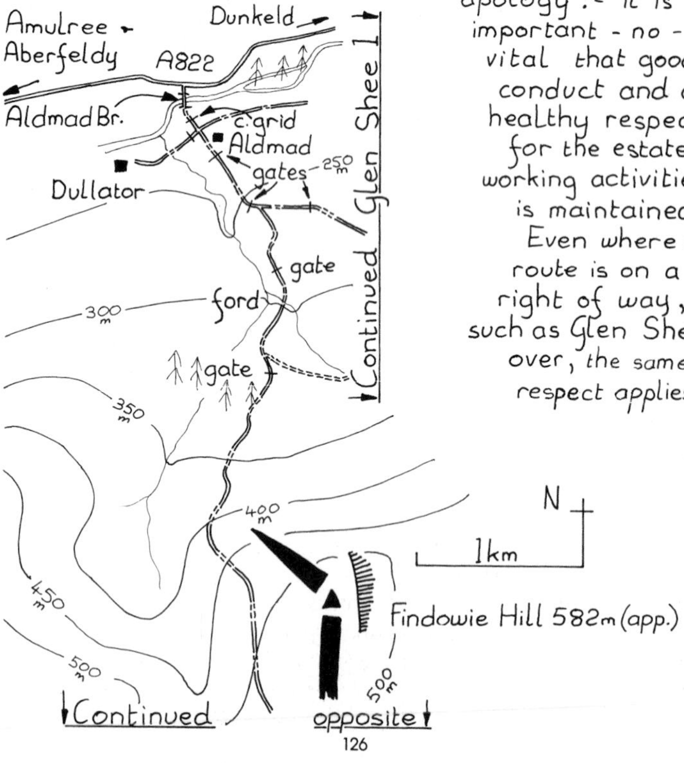

Continued Glen Shee 1

Continued opposite

Milton Burn 2

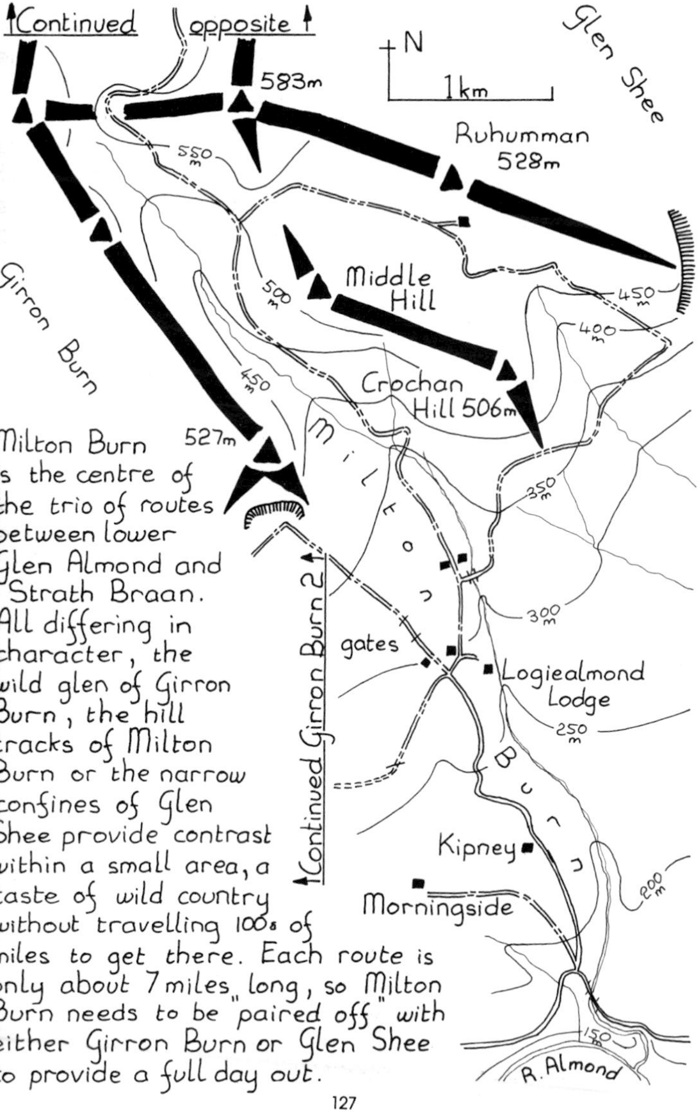

Milton Burn is the centre of the trio of routes between lower Glen Almond and Strath Braan. All differing in character, the wild glen of Girron Burn, the hill tracks of Milton Burn or the narrow confines of Glen Shee provide contrast within a small area, a taste of wild country without travelling 100s of miles to get there. Each route is only about 7 miles long, so Milton Burn needs to be "paired off" with either Girron Burn or Glen Shee to provide a full day out.

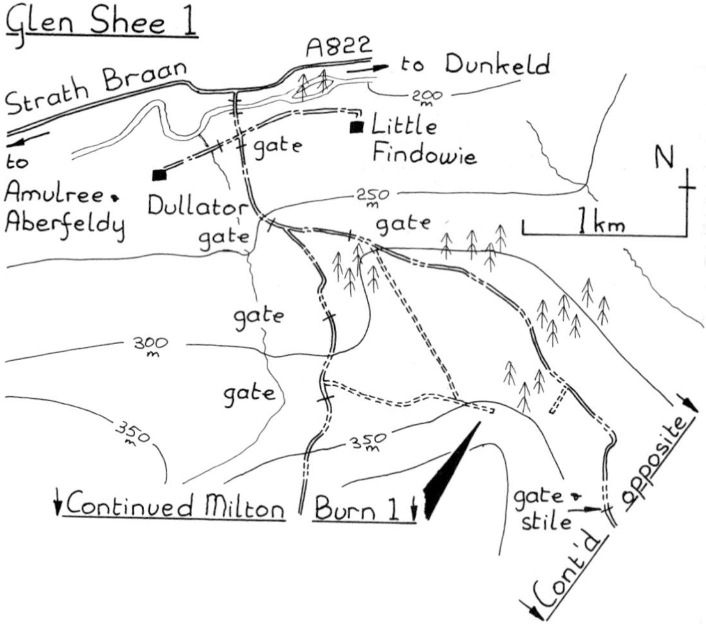
Glen Shee 1
A822
to Dunkeld
Strath Braan
200 m
Little Findowie
gate
to Amulree Aberfeldy
Dullator
250 m
gate
gate
N
1km
gate
300 m
gate
350 m
350 m
Continued Milton Burn 1
gate stile
Cont'd opposite

Glen Shee

Glen Shee 2

The track through Glen Shee is excellent for either a walk or a cycle ride. Not too rough for any to be unridable, yet rough enough to be interesting, this makes a short ride from the public road at Little Glenshee to Strathbraan. Indeed, the only snag is the short length of this track at only 7·5 km or 5 miles end to end. Such a fine route deserves to be longer! This route *is* a right of way so refused access to either of the preceeding glens (Milton Burn and Girron Burn) need not result in complete disappointment! The tracks X and Y below, are alas out-of-bounds for both walkers and cyclists alike - "farm track only - no public footpath", shame!!

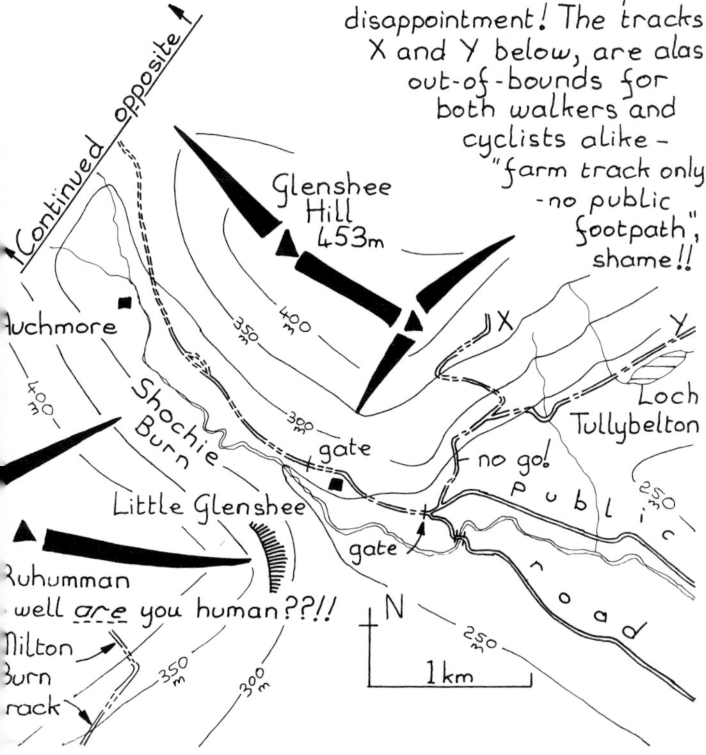

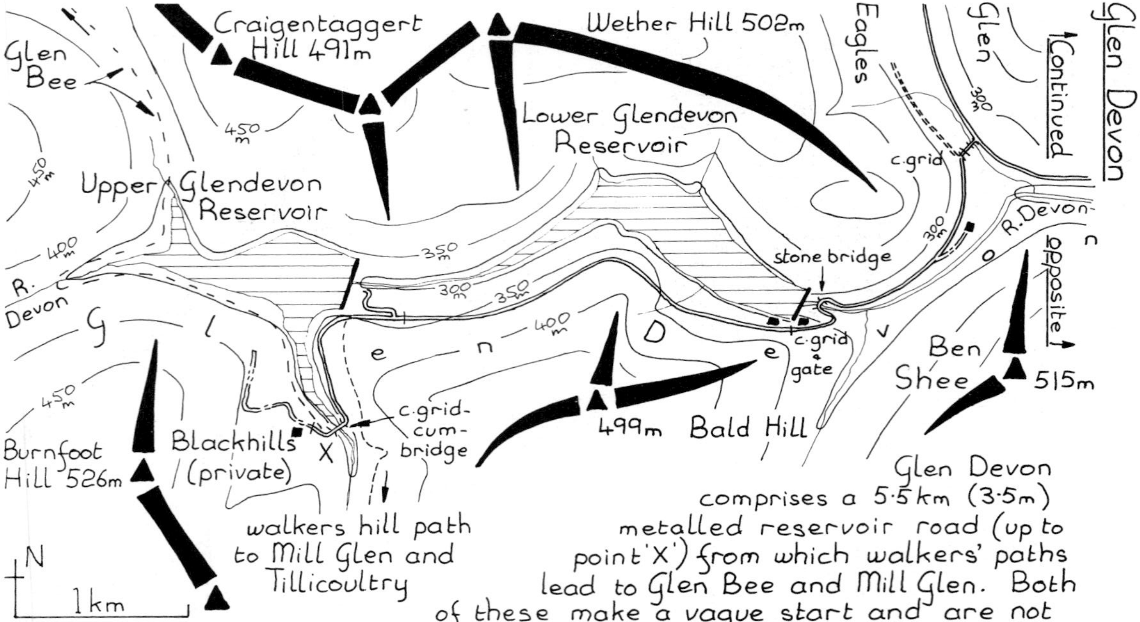

Glen Devon comprises a 5·5km (3·5m) metalled reservoir road (up to point 'X') from which walkers' paths lead to Glen Bee and Mill Glen. Both of these make a vague start and are not therefore fully mapped here. Glen Devon provides a dead easy bike ride or a walkers' introduction to a number of equally easy but pleasant hill walks on the rounded Ochil Hills.

Glen Sherup

Having explored Glen Devon and discovered it's still only lunchtime the remainder of the day and any remaining energy may be spent up Glen Sherup. This lopsided glen with its forest all on one side and its reservoir in the bottom demonstrates what a mess we can make of our environment, even with 'natural' elements like trees and water! It is, nevertheless, a decent track with some views looking down towards Glen Devon.

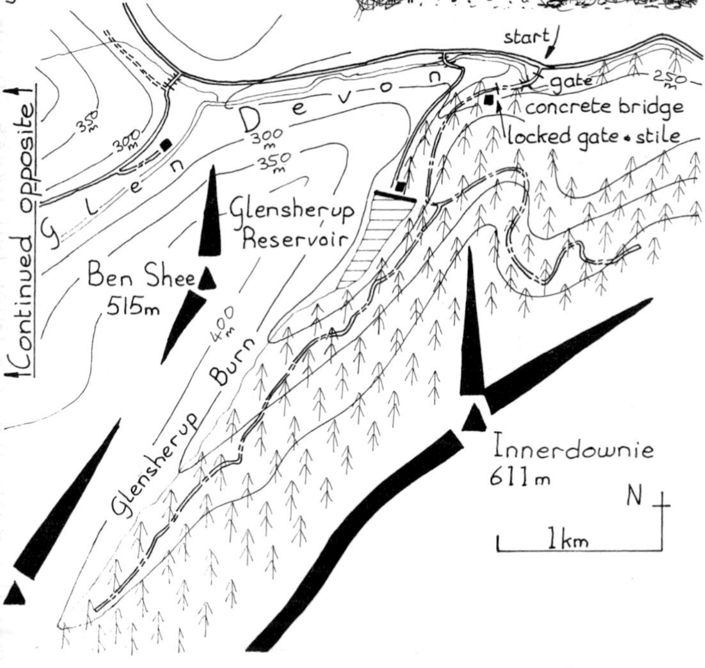

Carron Valley 1

Carron Valley Reservoir lies just a few miles south west of Stirling between the Fintry Hills and Touch Hills to the north and the Kilsyth Hills in the south. This is not The Trossachs and is somewhat detached, geographically, from the rest of this guide. However a useful area of

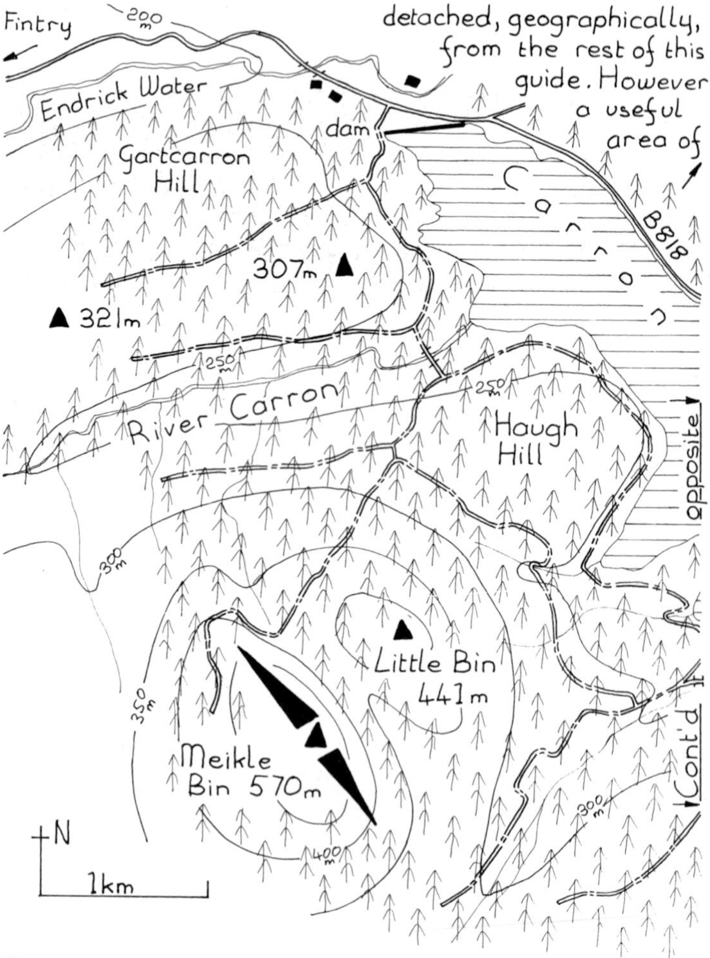

tracks provides both walks and off-road cycling, free from the restrictions imposed elsewhere due to the Forestry Commission encouraging these activities. Carron Valley is an accessible haven away from the mayhem of the nearby cities.

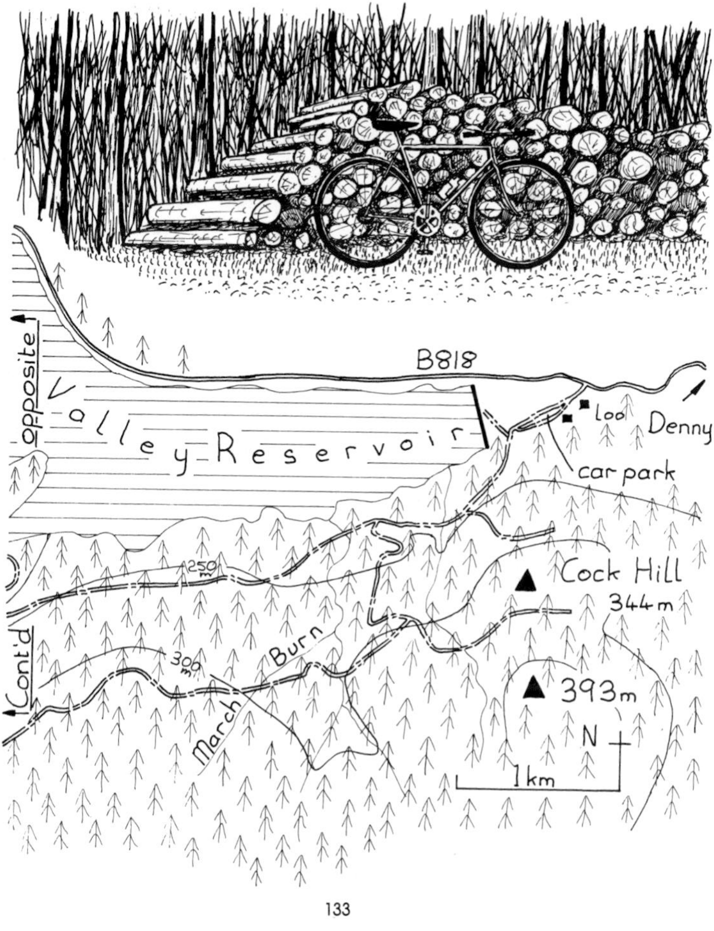

Link Routes

The link routes shown demonstrate how long through routes are made up from the various page maps. Variations can be planned using further adjacent routes but these should provide a basis for extended exploration.

Loch Ard to Loch Tay.

Link Route 1

Loch Ard to Loch Tay provides a fine long route virtually all on good tracks and with very little road (thro' Aberfoyle only). Total distance from the Drymen road entry to L. Ard Forest to Ardeonaig via Callander is 100km (63 m) app.

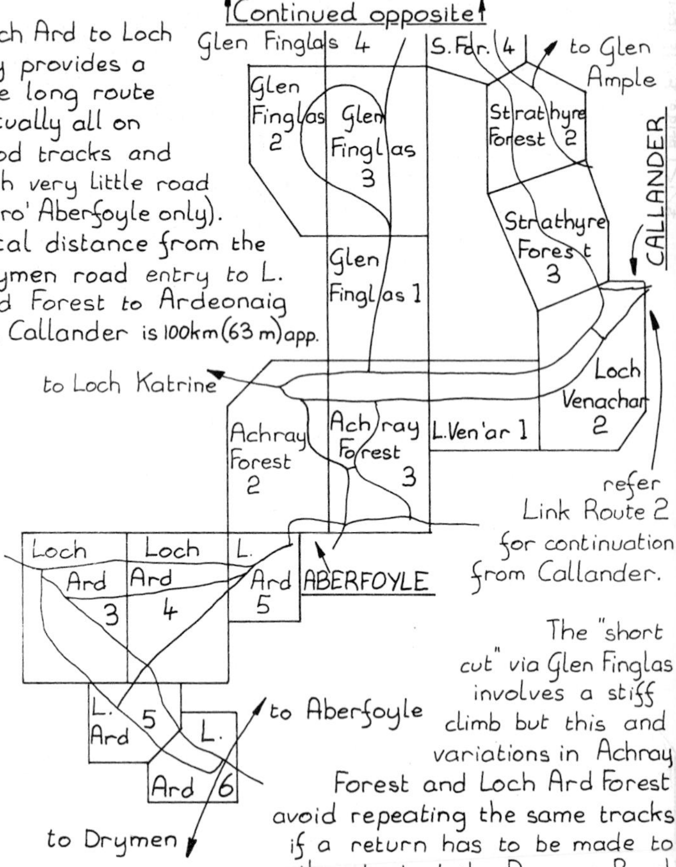

refer Link Route 2 for continuation from Callander.

The "short cut" via Glen Finglas involves a stiff climb but this and variations in Achray Forest and Loch Ard Forest avoid repeating the same tracks if a return has to be made to the start at the Drymen Road.

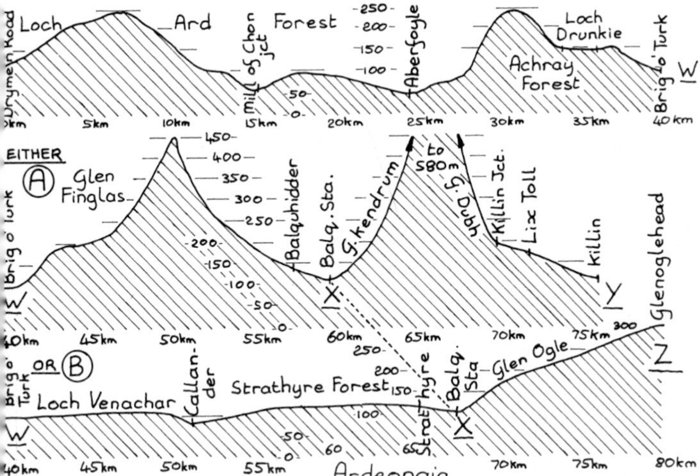

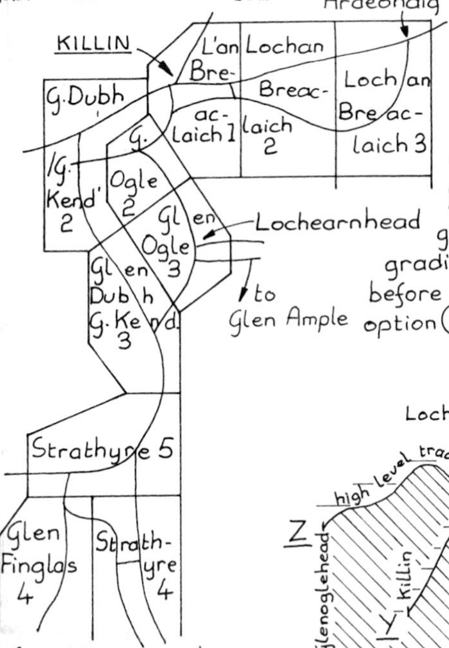

Cont'd opposite

Note:- distances are approximate due to the many possible variations. Link Y-Z is 10km via Killin Junction and Lix Toll at even gradient. Track/path grading should be studied before setting off. The easy option (B) above is the best of the two routes.

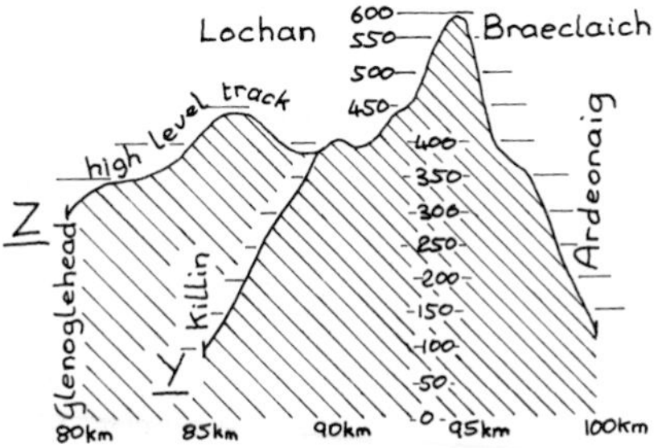

Loch Tay to Callander — Link Route 2

A through route with track, path and public road. The map pages below require careful study before setting out. Connections to 'Link Route 1' at Ardeonaig and Callander make the combination of the two routes suitable for an extended tour of several days' length

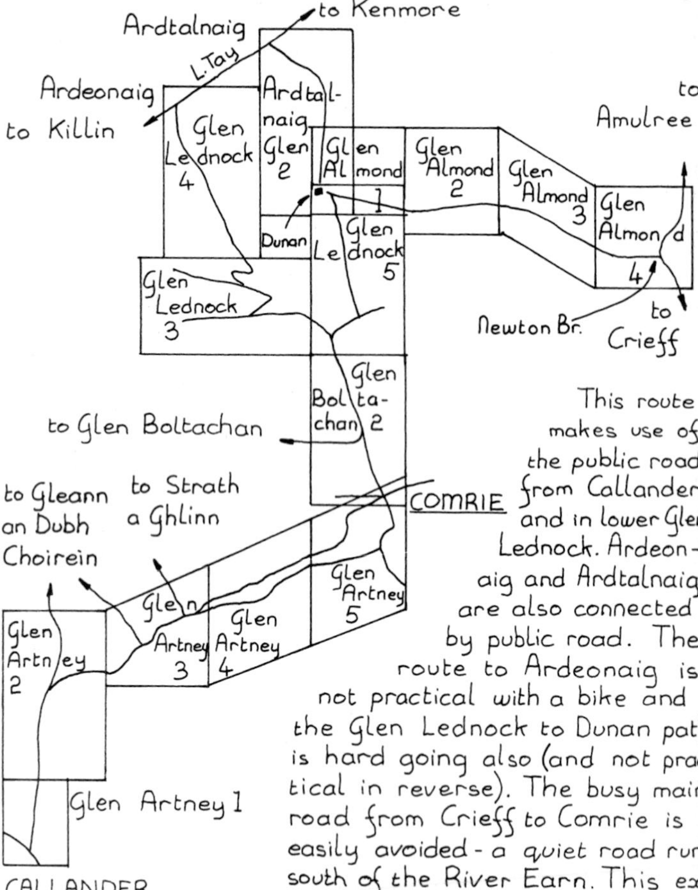

This route makes use of the public road from Callander and in lower Glen Lednock. Ardeonaig and Ardtalnaig are also connected by public road. The route to Ardeonaig is not practical with a bike and the Glen Lednock to Dunan path is hard going also (and not practical in reverse). The busy main road from Crieff to Comrie is easily avoided - a quiet road runs south of the River Earn. This extends options for a 'circular' route.

When combined, link routes 1 and 2 add up to a tour of about 220km or 140 miles which, together with the option of exploring side-glens should provide enough for a self-planned backpacking or off road cycling tour, away from the crowds tramping up the West Highland Way (but not completely tourist-free!). This route is also more suited to cycling than the W.H.W. The best start/finish points are Drymen or Aberfoyle. The circuit deserves a name:- "The Trossachs Tour"??

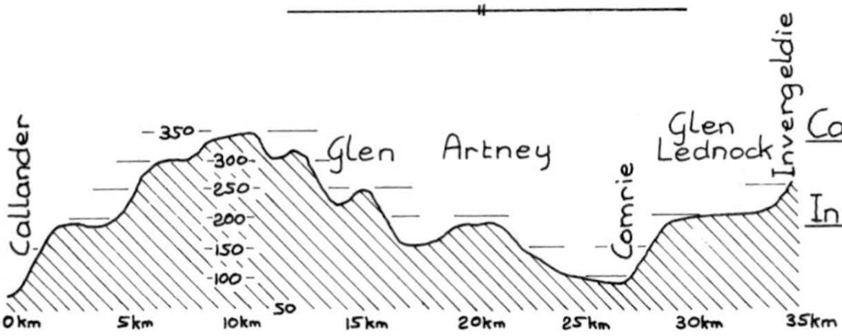

Callander to Invergeldie

Invergeldie to Ardeonaig

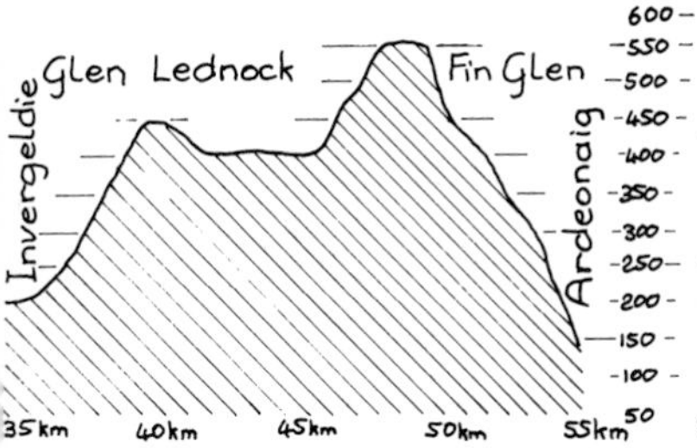

Invergeldie to Dunan

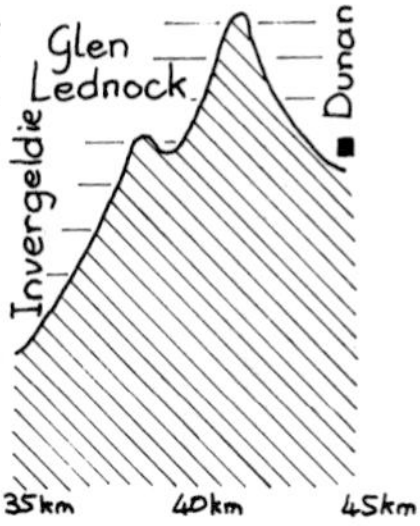

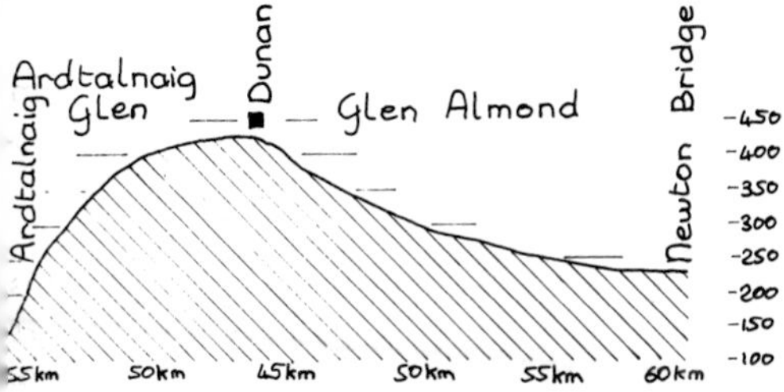

Ardtalnaig to Newton Bridge

Callander to Lochearnhead

Link Route 3

A committing walk, *not* a bike ride, of some 25km/16 miles (or 16km/10 miles road to road). Care should be taken in route-finding over the col at the head of Glen Vorlich as the path is vague in places. An escape route exists from the ruin of Dubh Chorein, down the glen of the same name. This saves the second climb but Auchinner, in Glen Artney, is still 6·5km (or 4 miles) distant - and in the wrong glen! Those with surplus energy may wish to incorporate Stuc a' Chroin (972m) and Ben Vorlich (985m) adding substantially to the ascent but not the distance making this a fine, but serious, walk incorporating both mountain and glen.

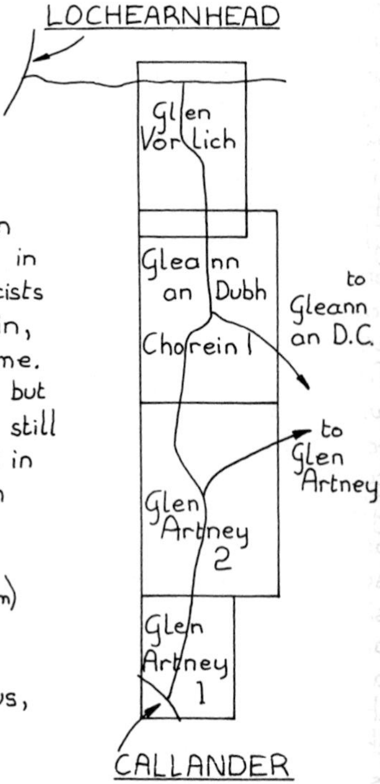

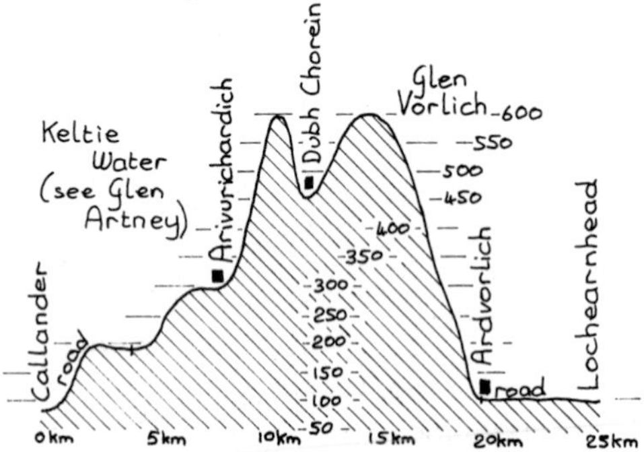

Now that Book 4 is complete each book, each geographical area covered can be seen to have its own individual character:- The Cairngorm Glens explores the forests and perimeter tracks of the area with some exciting sorties into the centre of this unique mountain area. (Sadly this region also has the worst of the man-made scars in the shape of badly built tracks and ski-ing development - why do we spoil that which is most sacred?) I digress; The Atholl Glens explores the less mountainous area south and west of the Cairngorms, an area of forest and long, lonely glens leading through remote country with scenic gems around Blair Atholl and Loch Tummel; The Glens of Rannoch covered some real wilderness, long committing routes tied together by rail almost as much as by road - an area for the connoisseur of wild places. But what of The Trossach Glens? A beautiful scenic area of mountain, forest and loch.... and disused railways, leaving a slightly sad feeling of what life was once like, with panting steam engines toiling over the hills of Strathyre and Glenoglehead. Now we have panting cyclists - a new lease of life for a part of our infrastructure that is too valuable to lose - and a lot cleaner than the old steam engines! (Well a bit!) The Trossachs is very much a tourist area, as demonstrated by Dochart Bridge which seems to have a coach party glued to it all summer, oblivious to passing traffic, especially bikes! A sharp contrast with Rannoch, but it is good to see so many people enjoying their holidays by bike and on foot instead of polluting the place aimlessly driving about. I still have my doubts about "experiencing the forest" by driving around it at Loch Drunkie. Whilst on the subject of forests I must not forget to thank the Forestry Commission in Aberfoyle for their help and encouragement in mapping the forest tracks; also the Central Scotland Water Development Board for information relating to Loch Turret and Strathclyde Water for their approval of the section on Loch Ard Forest. The attitude of the above organizations is refreshing. If only Scotrail were as cycle-friendly - then the railways that remain open would be almost as much use to the cyclist as those that were closed thirty years ago!

On a personal note, 1994 has been a year of great change. The lure of the Highlands with its high mountains, lonely glens and quiet roads proved irresistible so, when the opportunity presented itself, your author moved lock, stock and barrel to be in the midst of this grandeur. We are indeed fortunate to live in a country where such wonderful scenery exists and also where this freedom of movement is possible. The rat-race already feels to be well behind me. The greed based scenario of more-bigger-better fails to impress me and life is much more civilized in a society based upon human values with good old fashioned manners instead of pure consumerism - the "I must have" syndrome. Materialistic wealth is largely irrelevant with Glen Affric almost in the back garden. There is not the need to build a shield of possessions around oneself as protection from the self-generated stress of city life. This is replaced by a feeling of peace and freedom, far more valuable attributes!

I hope, through the pages of these books that my readers find some of that peace, solitude and time for reflection, in a way only possible in our wild places. If so, then in addition to providing a guide to where and how to go I would feel well satisfied with my work. Get on with it - enough of this philosophy! This is supposed to be a guide book - on yer bike and off to the Argyll Glens!